黃河

THE YELLOW RIVER

A 5000 YEAR JOURNEY THROUGH CHINA

HIROYUKI USAMI

中華有蛟龍
其名曰黃河
尾擊青海遠
口吐烈焰多
奔騰歸渤海
壯哉我黃河

With its tail lashing the Qinghai plateau, and its mouth breathing fire into the Gulf of Bohai, the Huanghe is indeed the dragon river of China.

HIROYUKI USAMI

A 5000 YEAR JOURNEY THROUGH CHINA

KEVIN SINCLAIR

BASED ON THE ACCLAIMED BBC TELEVISION DOCUMENTARY

WEIDENFELD AND NICOLSON
LONDON

Above: **O**ld tales live again on a village stage in Wei in Shanxi province when a traditional theatrical group comes to town.

Endpapers: **A**nxious faces turn to watch the rising waters as peasants hurry to repair earthworks in *Building a Dyke against the Threatening Waves of the Yellow River,* an anonymous painting from around 1689.
MUSEE GUIMET, PARIS/AMERICAN HERITAGE

Page 1: **A**cross the lonely high steppes of the Ordos, a nomad makes soulful music on a horsehead harp.

Page 2: **T**wilight brings a golden sheen to the aptly named Yellow River.

Pages 4–5: **A**s everywhere, a marriage is a time to get dressed up. It's the same on the Roof of the World, where these Matau nomads take advantage of the occasion to put on their finest clothes.
YASUHIRO HAYASHI

Chapter openers: **S**cenes from *Spring Festival on the River* by Chang Tse-tuan.
METROPOLITAN MUSEUM OF ART/AMERICAN HERITAGE

First published in Great Britain in 1987 by
George Weidenfeld & Nicolson Limited
91 Clapham High Street
London SW4 7TA

Produced by
Intercontinental Publishing Corporation Limited
4th Floor, 69 Wyndham Street, Central Hong Kong
Telex 83499 PPA HX; Fax 5-8101683
A member of the Weldon-Hardie Group of Companies
Sydney • Auckland • Hong Kong • London • Chicago

ISBN 0 297 79231 8

Associate publisher: John Owen
Editorial director: Elaine Russell
Project coordinators: Patricia Davis, Sheena Coupe
Editor: Beverley Barnes
Captions: Kevin Sinclair, Carson Creagh
Index: Dianne Regtop
Picture research: Douglas Tunstell, Laurie Platt Winfrey
Picture editors: Mary-Dawn Earley, Shigeki Ohyama
Map and illustrations: John Rissetto
Calligraphy: Wong Chiu Tung
Production: Kate Smyth, Sue Tickner

Design John Bull, The Book Design Co.

English translation rights arranged with
Japan Broadcast Publishing Co Ltd
through Japan UNI Agency, Inc, Tokyo

Typeset by Amazing Faces, Sydney, Australia
Production by Mandarin Offset, Hong Kong
Printed by Toppan Printing Company, Hong Kong
Printed in Hong Kong

A KEVIN WELDON PRODUCTION

Contents

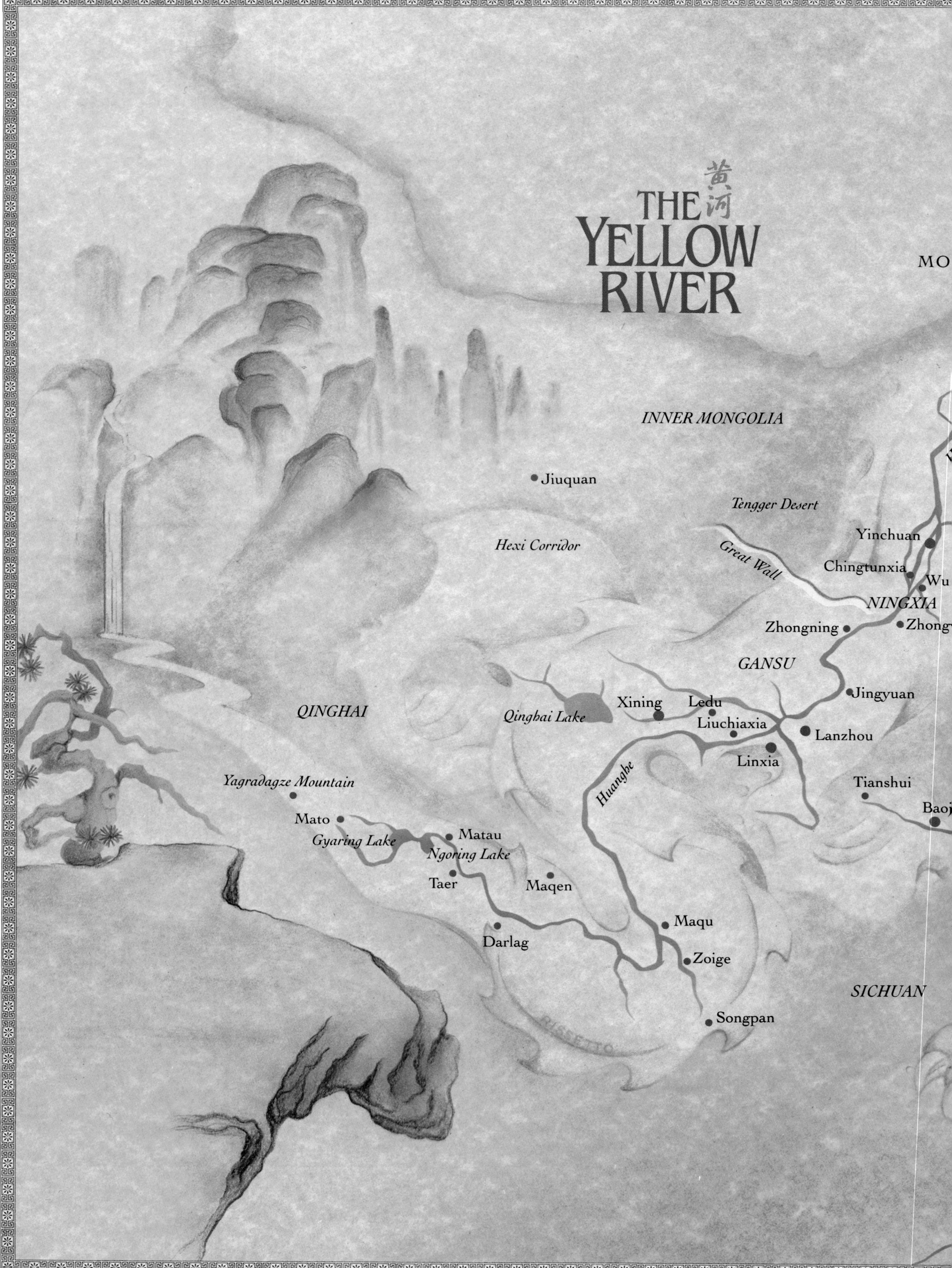
黄河
THE YELLOW RIVER
MO
INNER MONGOLIA
Jiuquan
Tengger Desert
Hexi Corridor
Great Wall
Yinchuan
Chingtunxia
Wu
NINGXIA
Zhongning
Zhong
GANSU
Jingyuan
Xining
Ledu
QINGHAI
Qinghai Lake
Liuchiaxia
Lanzhou
Linxia
Huanghe
Tianshui
Yagradagze Mountain
Baoj
Mato
Matau
Gyaring Lake
Ngoring Lake
Taer
Maqen
Maqu
Darlag
Zoige
SICHUAN
Songpan
RISSETTO

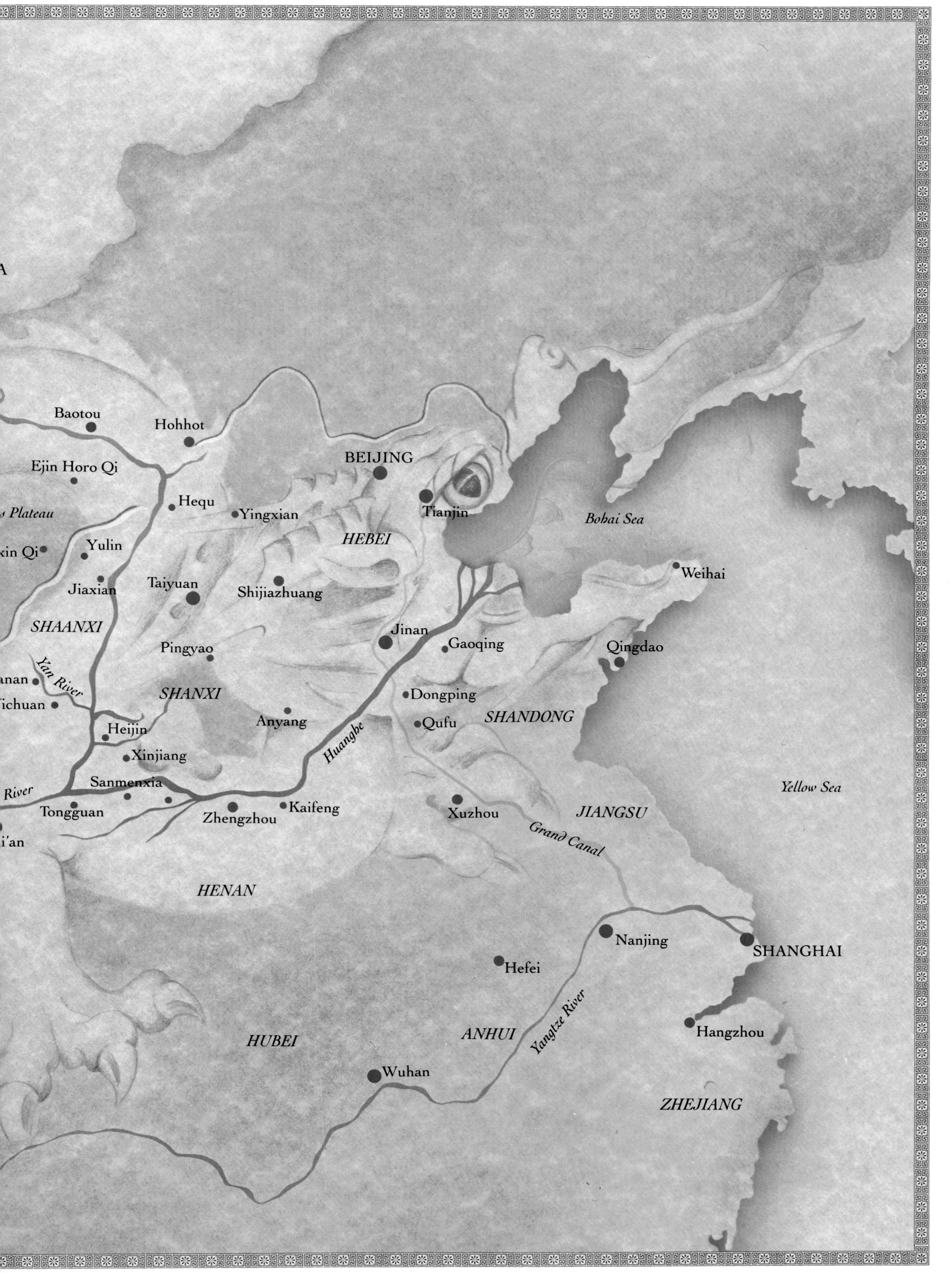
Baotou
Hohhot
Ejin Horo Qi
BEIJING
Tianjin
Hequ
Yingxian
Bohai Sea
HEBEI
Yulin
Weihai
Jiaxian
Taiyuan
Shijiazhuang
SHAANXI
Jinan
Gaoqing
Qingdao
Pingyao
Yan River
SHANXI
Dongping
Anyang
Qufu
SHANDONG
Heijin
Xinjiang
Huanghe
Sanmenxia
Yellow Sea
Tongguan
Zhengzhou
Kaifeng
Xuzhou
JIANGSU
Grand Canal
HENAN
Nanjing
SHANGHAI
Hefei
Yangtze River
Hangzhou
HUBEI
ANHUI
Wuhan
ZHEJIANG

HIROYUKI USAMI

序言

PREFACE

'WHOEVER CONTROLS the Yellow River controls China', claimed the legendary Yu who, according to tradition, founded the Xia dynasty in the second millennium before Christ and tamed the river to conserve its waters. The Yellow River – to the Chinese, the Huanghe – is both the source and the destroyer of life. Rising deep in the country's interior, high above sea level in the province of Qinghai, the river loops and twists across desert wastes and loess lands before crossing the North China Plain on its way to the Gulf of Bohai. On its 5000-kilometre journey to the sea it flows through mountain passes, marshlands, deserts, steppes and plateaus. At times it is broad and peaceful, at others it rages violently through canyons and chasms. It traverses harshly uncompromising and uninhabited landscapes as well as busy industrial and urban areas. In places its banks are home to nomadic tribes who still live by ancient traditions and customs and in others modern technology is being used to harness its power to provide dams, hydroelectricity and irrigation schemes.

The Huanghe is a powerful symbol in the mythology of China; it is the dragon of Chinese legend, the river of sorrows, the cradle of civilisation, the country's historic heartland. From its huge basin, which has an area of 750 000 square kilometres, sprang one of the world's great civilisations. Bones from the Palaeolithic era – perhaps a million years old – have been found near the river. Over five thousand years ago Neolithic people settled by its shores to grow crops and to fish; their painted pottery is still admired for its symmetry and the beauty of its execution. Since then it has nurtured the great dynasties of China – The Shang and Zhou, the Qin, Han, Tang and northern Song.

This book is a record of and a tribute to that mighty river.

Sheep are driven to market in Wuzhong, on the southern bank of the Huanghe.

黄河及其子孫

A RIVER AND ITS PEOPLE

AT THE FOOT of Mount Mang not far from Zhengzhou in Henan province stands a white marble statue. It portrays a woman gently comforting a baby. The woman is the Huanghe, the Yellow River, which slides past the foot of the mountain on its way 1000 kilometres downriver to the Gulf of Bohai. The infant receiving such loving care represents the Chinese people. Mother and child, the river and the race; it was on the banks of the waterway somewhere along this stretch of the river that the people who later became the Chinese first made their appearance on the stage of history. Throughout their long existence, the richness and waters of the Huanghe have provided the vital means to sustain them. The statue illustrates to the hundreds of thousands of visitors who every year visit Mount Mang the closeness of the relationship between the river and the people for whom it has provided succour for countless generations. But the swirling yellow waters have brought disaster as well as survival.

Today, developed as a recreation area where people can view the meandering Yellow River from hills topped with pagodas and monuments, Mount Mang in many ways contains in its small area much of the essence of the waterway it overlooks. The mountain is made of loess, and it is this fine dusty grit, windborne over half a continent, that has formed much of the drainage area of the Huanghe. It is the loess, carried by the river down from the uplands in the form of silt, that has over millions of years created the flat arable North China Plain. And it is the con-

*L*ate afternoon sun glints on the river as it courses over the high plains of Qinghai. Near the town of Darlag, the stream looks more like the Silver River than the Yellow River: hundreds of kilometres from its source the waters still run clear and fresh.

YASUHIRO HAYASHI

A seagull's shed feather points to the mouth of the Huanghe. Left high and dry by retreating tides, the feather rests on silt patterned by the current.

tinuing dumping of loess silt by floodwaters that has caused the Yellow River to build up its bed; now it flows along on top of a pyramid of consolidated silt, and when the waters break through the dykes they spread in immense lakes over the farmland. That is when millions have died of drowning and famine. And that is why throughout history the Huanghe has been known as 'China's Sorrow'.

Mount Mang has many other lessons as well as those carried in the loess of which it is built. On a distant peak, overlooking the mighty waterway to which he seems to beckon, is a statue to Yu the Great. When he took the throne forty-two centuries ago and founded the Xia dynasty, Yu attempted to control the seasonal rampages of the river. He watches over it still. Later rulers also climbed the eroded gullies of Mount Mang to ponder the river, consider its threats, contemplate its promise. One of the most famous modern portraits taken along the Huanghe, reproduced endlessly in China, shows the late Chairman Mao Zedong sitting on one of the peaks looking down at the serpentine channels winding out over the plains. In those days, a bridge spanned the river and its huge floodplain. Today there are two bridges, one for road traffic and one for rail, carrying the produce and manufactures of Henan over the waters.

Mount Mang holds lessons for the future as well as messages from the past. When planners in the late 1970s decided to turn the area into an historical park where people could learn about the river, they also started to protect the hills from the vicious erosion which had eaten into the loess flanks. Today, the steep slopes are terraced to prevent swift runoffs from summer rain cutting into the fibre of the land. Newly planted, deep-rooted fruit trees and hardy pines will help to bind the land with their root systems. Upstream, vast areas larger than many European nations have been similarly terraced and planted to prevent the erosion that leads to silting of the river which in grim turn leads to flooding. Mount Mang demonstrates in miniature many of the problems and promises of the entire Huanghe. The view of the Yellow River also illustrates vividly why the waterway bears its name. By the time it reaches the plains, the waters carry an immense load of silt, sixty times more than the waters of the Mississippi. The ochre mud washed down from the ravaged highlands gives the river a hue that ranges from a golden glow under the sun to a sullen greyish tone under winter snow clouds.

The two bridges that cross the wide floodplain stretch so far into the hazy distance that even from the pagodas atop Mount Mang the far ends cannot be seen. Bridges are a symbol of progress on the river, rare ones right up to modern times. Until a few years ago, crossings high upstream were commonly made on rafts of inflated hides. Further along the course, there were ferries. On the unpredictable lower stretches, sometimes in full flood, at other times without enough water to float a boat, getting across the Huanghe was throughout history both uncertain and dangerous.

YASUHIRO HAYASHI

*F*ace weatherbeaten by ten thousand sunrises, the captain of a river mouth ferry squints into the winter horizon as he steers downstream. Many thousands of men and women make their livelihoods navigating the waters of the Huanghe.

*T*he features of this headman from a Shaanxi village bear evidence of the many peoples who have marched over the Huanghe valley south of the Great Wall.

Overleaf

*T*he treeless and windswept desolation of *Hua shi xia*, or 'flower stone valley' southwest of Xining, belies its romantic name. In spring, however, wildflowers provide rich grazing for herds of yaks and hardy Tibetan sheep.
YASUHIRO HAYASHI

The first recorded link over the river was built in the Ming dynasty (1368–1644) by a general who ordered a pontoon strung across the river near Lanzhou so his army could march over the water to do battle with threatening barbarians. This structure of twenty-four connected boats was known as the First Huanghe Bridge Under Heaven, a hazardous piece of primitive engineering battered by summer floods and winter icefloes. In all China's long history, according to records kept by the national government in Beijing, not one permanent bridge spanned the waterway until 1905. By 1912, there were three of them, many hundreds of kilometres apart at Lanzhou, Zhengzhou and Jinan. The steel crossing at Lanzhou cost the Qing empire 360 000 taels of silver and was built by a German company. It lasted until a new five-lane highway bridge 300 metres long was built in 1979. From the time the imposing structure at Lanzhou was erected until 1950, no new bridge was thrown over the Huanghe. Today more than fifty-four bridges cross the river. The highest is a 'bridge in-the-sky' at Lake Ngoring in Qinghai province where a span 80 metres long crosses the young waterway. A further 40 kilometres downstream, the second bridge over the Huanghe carries the highway linking Qinghai and Sichuan. As the river gets bigger, the bridges get longer. The rail bridge that strides on seventy-one arches over the floodplain at Zhengzhou is 3 kilometres long. In Shandong province the rail bridge at Luokou is 5.7 kilometres in length.

It is far, far from these plains that the Yellow River begins its story. That starts more than 4000 kilometres upriver on the remote and icy plateau of Qinghai. Indeed, for many thousands of years the very birthplace of the Huanghe was a mystery to those who dwelt along the lower banks. It was, simply, The River. Where it rose was unknown, a matter of conjecture, rumour, speculation, legend. Only in 1985 did a team from the River Source Research Party of the Yellow River Conservancy Commission plot the definitive source of the highest of the headwaters. Today, Chinese satellites launched from pads in Xinjiang can plot with ease the vast sweep of the river as it cuts across the entire breadth of the land. From the vantage point of space, the river writhes, curls back on itself, bends and gyrates in wild changes of course as it spills wildly down from the highland plateau through the tortured loess uplands of Gansu, in its great bend that sweeps north to Mongolia, down through the gullies and ravines of Shaanxi-Shanxi to the rich flatlands of the North China Plain. The course, sketched roughly on a map, looks like the outline of an angry, arch-backed dragon. The mouth spits fury at the Gulf of Bohai, the tail lashes the Bayan Har mountains 5464 kilometres upstream.

Little coincidence, perhaps, that the river's course should resemble the shape of a dragon. For many centuries, superstitious farmers believed the Huanghe was occupied by a dragon, controlled by a fearsome beast. The water and silt bring life to the peasants; for centuries they still feared it. With good reason. The unpredictable, turbulent stream was no gentle servant. Elevated in its silty bed high above

WILLIAM NG

*Y*oung men practise the ancient skills of kung-fu in the fields near Kaifeng. They study the art under the tutelage of the monks of the nearby Shaolin Temple.

SEIGO OTSUKA

Standing ten metres high and weighing 150 tonnes, the statue of the legendary emperor, Yu the Great, symbolising flood control and mastery over the Huanghe dominates this mountain lookout north of Luoyang. The mountain itself, once barren, has now become fertile as a result of irrigation.

the level of the plains, it could rise suddenly after heavy summer rains and overflow its banks. The floods destroyed homes, killed millions of people in China's history. The resulting famines, caused because crops were destroyed by water and silt, killed millions more. China's Sorrow; seldom was a river better named.

The river was also parent of the Chinese people, as the statue at Mount Mang makes so plain. Scientists have used carbon-dating techniques to prove that individuals who were forerunners of modern human beings lived by the banks of the Huanghe about 850 000 years ago. Stable, settled agricultural societies rose there over the centuries, and by 5000 years ago mankind could make pottery and decorate it finely, build fortified settlements, plough and grow millet and other grains in sufficient quantity to begin a civilisation. The fields were watered from the Yellow River. Its murky liquid was the lifeblood of the Chinese people.

HIROYUKI USAMI

With Ramadan at an end, Hui women prepare traditional delicacies for a feast. The lamb and vegetable-stuffed dumplings, reflecting a marriage of Chinese cuisine and Islamic dietary dictates, will be eagerly awaited by the faithful who have fasted for a month.

Today, the river flows through nine provinces and autonomous regions on its twisting journey from the highlands to the sea. Passing over Qinghai, skirting Sichuan, cutting across Gansu, the river then flows northwards through the Ningxia Hui Autonomous Region, eastwards through Inner Mongolia, and forms the border between Shaanxi and Shanxi before entering the Great Northern Plain and winding through Henan and Shandong to the Gulf of Bohai. On its way, it drops 4500 metres from mountain to sea-level, collects forty major tributaries, hundreds of streams, thousands of creeks. In the 752 443 square kilometres of its drainage area, there dwell 120 million people. One way or another, directly or indirectly, their lives depend on the Huanghe. In addition to its waters, the river has many riches.Minerals stud the banks in Qinghai, gold is washed in Ningxia, huge chemical factories line the banks in Lanzhou, sprawling steel plants in Baotou, Inner Mongolia, and the historic old capitals in the heartland – Xi'an, Luoyang, Zhengzhou, Kaifeng – are today major centres of manufacturing and industry. Shanxi province sits atop an almost-limitless amount of high-grade coal, and where the waters of the Gulf of Bohai turn an ochre hue because of the silt from the Yellow River scores of massive rigs suck up the black gold of oil.

More than natural treasures lie buried in the deep beds of loess that cover the plains. There is also the heritage of a people and a nation, for it was in modern Henan province that the Chinese people were spawned by the Yellow River. Relics of a hundred centuries have been found here, precious legacy of a forgotten past. Along the banks, kingdoms rose, empires flowered, invaders rode, dynasties floundered. The river deposited thick layers of silt over the cities and encampments of successive civilisations, preserving them in cloying earth. Protected from natural decay and human despoliation, treasures of the past are being discovered today. There is still much to learn of the past locked into the natural vaults of the earth, anthropologists and archaeologists believe, because it was in the cities along the plain that successive Chinese civilisations seem to have burst into vital and glorious life.

*H*ome for a holiday from his devotions, novice monk Li Hua returns to spend a few days with his family at their home in Guide. After a reunion with his parents, brothers, sisters and friends, Li Hua will go back to the Taer Temple to continue his studies aimed at preparing him for a priestly life as a monk.

Almost every aspect of culture, science and learning equated with the growth of society can be traced to the lower stretch of the river from Shaanxi to the sea. Taoist and Confucian belief was born here. So was the study of humans and their environment, which gave rise to encyclopaedias of herbal medicine in the Song dynasty and acupuncture. Architecture developed here, with foundations laid for buildings twenty centuries ago that carry the familiar upswerving eaves so popular today. Above all, what we recognise today as the Chinese language in both its spoken and written forms can trace its beginning back directly to earlier civilisations along the Huanghe. It is in calligraphy that Chinese scholars and artists traditionally take greatest pride, and the earliest examples of surviving characters come carved on horn or bone or tortoiseshell excavated in archaeological digs in Henan; these date back to 2000 BC. From writing came the vital twin skills of papermaking and printing; reproduction of written messages using woodblock printing was highly developed in the Tang dynasty (AD 618–907).

The sound of music floated early over the Yellow River; the seven-stringed zither is at least 3000 years old, and the *pipa,* a pear-shaped lute with four strings, was being played in its present form in Kaifeng seventeen centuries ago just as it is played today in concert halls throughout China. Poetry, one of the highest art forms, was much prized in ancient dynasties. Even when writing of love and passion, poets often turned to the Huanghe and its tributaries to illustrate their point, as did the writer of this example taken from the Scripture of Poetry of the Zhou dynasty.

Qi's waters swell and flood
Our carriage hangings are wet.
Nothing I've done has not been straight
Nothing of yours but bent
You set no limits to what you did
– Man of too many inner selfs.

Mathematics, the sciences, the study of the earth, animals, the heavens, religion, the arts, drama, music, opera, fine pottery, cuisine, language, agriculture . . . almost every aspect of what we now think of as Chinese culture, the Chinese way of life, developed into forms we can recognise today on the banks of the Yellow River centuries ago. So, too, did the science of hydrology, the study of rivers and their ways. More than 4200 years ago, rulers along the Huanghe appointed officials to high office to study how best to tame this lethal source of life, at times a friend, at others a malignant foe. It is a study that continues today with scientists of many disciplines continuing research into how best to control and make use of the perilous endowments of the Huanghe.

It is a changing river. Its headwaters sparkle amid ice and snow and sunshine as they run through crystal lakes and alpine meadows. Further down, burdened

HIROYUKI USAMI

*T*heir home a boat, this fishing family spend their lives on the waters of Dongping Lake. Even afloat, they grow flowers planted in an endless supply of rich silt scooped from the lake bed.

with huge loads of silt, it churns massively through gorges, chokes hydroelectric dams, boils over rapids. Then, miraculously, as it runs between enormous earthworks designed to withstand gigantic floods, the dreaded Huanghe for long months of the year dwindles to a turgid stream. It meanders aimlessly through huge beds of silt solidifying into mud, a modest waterway almost lost in its own floodplain 5 kilometres wide. At Kaifeng, in Henan province, the river runs between dykes 13 kilometres apart; from the air the watery strands twist like tangled yellow noodles over this broad floodplain. More than half the water has by this stage been taken from the river for human use. So much has been drawn off to water thirsty fields upstream that the lower course in Shandong province is often dry. This is a perverse state of affairs for a river whose name is synonymous with flooding. But those dykes are needed when the river runs full. This can happen suddenly, with a shocking swiftness following cloudbursts in the loess plateau of Shaanxi or Shanxi. That is why the Chinese nation spends a significant fortune every year continually building up the dykes along the final 1000 kilometres of the river as it crosses the plains.

Left

Contemplating a lifetime of prayer past and an eternity of prayer to come in other incarnations, an old monk wrapped in well-worn robes murmurs the chants of his faith in the Lesser Temple of the Golden Roof near Xining.

WILLIAM NG

Early morning along the city moat, Xi'an. As an important and prosperous city for many centuries, Xi'an has retained many of its traditional buildings and the classically regular street alignment. Four walls once protected the city.

古文明之搖籃

The Cradle of Civilisation

The history of China is the tale of the Yellow River. The Chinese people evolved along its banks before the Stone Age, coalesced into tribes which caught fish that swam in its shallows and hunted animals that drank its waters, developed into crude farmers who watered their rough fields of barley with droplets scooped up in skins. The river and the people are involved inextricably, moving together in history as certainly as the Huanghe flows towards the sea.

Scientists believe that early human-like creatures eked out an existence along the loess banks of the Yellow River as long as 850 000 years ago. Scraps of fossilised bone bearing scratch marks that could have been made by human teeth give the vaguest of clues. Shards of bone help anthropologists to build up a vague jigsaw portrait of a primitive forefather.

About 5000 years ago the tribes at various spots along the valley in the area of what is now Henan province had developed stable, prospering societies. Historical fact is woven with legend and folklore about these ancestors of the collective Chinese past. As with biblical figures from the birth of the Judeo-Christian era, several figures tend to meld into one identity giving rise to reputed reigns of some of the early rulers of more than a century.

The earliest date on which historians can settle with any scholarly accuracy is 2852 BC when T'ai Hao Fuh Hi ruled on the banks of the river near present-day Kaifeng. This shadowy father of the early Chinese is credited with forming the

*G*aily decorated riverboats are prepared for the annual Dragon Festival, during which the irascible dragon who ruled the Huanghe was placated with displays of fireworks, music, wine and celebrations.

very basis of the society that has ever since stubbornly resisted all attempts to change it; he organised clans and introduced family names. The name he took himself was that of Fung, meaning wind, the breeze that blows the loess which created the plains. In legend, ruler Fung blew much good, bequeathing to his subjects and to countless generations that followed them such benefits as stringed musical instruments, written memos and the institution of marriage. He taught not only hunting and fishing but also the rearing of animals. He was followed by Yen Ti Shen Nung, brought up in Henan, who lived most of his life downriver in the Shandong area. He invented the plough, recognised and encouraged the planting of the five types of grain, pioneered herbal medicine and is said to have reigned for 140 years.

According to Chinese legend, a poet fell in love with the goddess of the Huanghe, here represented with dragon feet. The original of this scroll dates from the fourth century; this copy was made in the twelfth or thirteenth century.

Then came Huang Ti, the revered Yellow Emperor, the towering figure still held in awe by Chinese as the premier founding father of the race. If only a small percentage of the achievements of this incredible ruler can be justly attributed to him, he must still have been a truly amazing man. He put down usurpers and

challengers, partly by the use of his invention of swords and shields. He invented the ministerial system of government and under his rule encouraged talented subordinates who devised writing, astronomical instruments and music. Other officials were placed in charge of pottery, the manufacture of arrows and the making of bows. The Yellow Emperor yoked oxen and caused horses to be laden to take the burden off the backs of men. He directed craftsmen to hollow out logs to make boats and sent them out to navigate the murky waters of the Huanghe. He devised a system of values for gems and metals, cast the first coins and promoted the study of medicine. His wife, Lei Tsu, was also busy; she taught his subjects how to rear silkworms, gather silk and make garments. Huang Ti also laid out the political outline of China, dividing his realm into provinces which could be more handily administered. Under his rule, and that of his successors, the people prospered. Agriculture was the focus of prime attention, but music, pottery, painting and other arts flourished. The embryonic Chinese empire spread up the Yellow River into Shanxi and downstream to Shandong.

SEIGO OTSUKA

*T*his savage watch-dragon stands guard on the roof of the Great Hall in the Taer Temple near Xining.

FREER GALLERY/AMERICAN HERITAGE

This bronze pot, decorative as well as useful, comes from the Boaji Museum collection.

Right
The introduction of Buddhism into China stimulated a fresh approach to art and the administration of the empire. The new philosophy also stimulated new methods of dealing with the perennial problem of China's turbulent and untamed rivers.

As the Chinese people increased, their domain extended. Inexorably, their armies occupied new lands. Barbarian tribes came under their sway, were incorporated into their civilisation. By 2000 BC the pattern that was to last 4000 years was established. It continues today. This spreading of Chinese influence, the flowering of art and culture, the increasing sophistication of rule, was based firmly on a sound agricultural base. And that was based on the waters of the Huanghe.

For most of the time, the river was benign. It rose and fell as snows melted in the unknown upper reaches and summer rains came to the middle courses. These rises could be generally anticipated. The river gave water that irrigated the crops. There was constant warfare with neighbouring tribes as the Chinese expansion continued. The annals of the Shang dynasty (sixteenth to eleventh century BC) make grim notations of the fluctuating fortunes of the state which rose and fell like the waters of the Yellow River on which it was based. In 1637 BC nobles of seventy-six surrounding states arrived at court to submit to Chinese rule. In 1557 BC, the southern barbarians of Lan arrived, not to meekly surrender but rather to plunder the country. In 1534 BC the river rose in disastrous flood, so severe that the capital had to be removed to the town (now lost) of Siang. 'Decay of the state', the surviving annals note ominously. Again in 1490 BC: 'confusion in the empire'. And in 1373 BC: 'Decay again'. But it was not all disaster. In 1293 BC three years of war with the Hun subtribe of Kuei-fang ended with them pledging submission. 'Then there was peace and prosperity', the ancient historians noted.

The stability and wealth created by these long periods of tranquillity was based on the strong backs of the peasant farmers. Atop this sturdy foundation of agricultural toil, successive emperors built temples to art, culture, cuisine and pleasure. But after more than six centuries of rule, the Shang dynasty began to rot from within. Decadence, corruption, cruelty and the pursuit of pleasure at court led to a loss of control. It was made worse by constant pressure from envious nomads and barbarians pressing in on every frontier. By 1124 BC Shang rule was so weak that 800 nobles met and withdrew their support of the emperor. The following year, after 644 years' reign by twenty-eight emperors, the Shang dynasty came to an end.

The capitals of the Shang rulers had shifted with the inclination of the emperors. Most now lost in time, the sites of the court ranged from Shandong to Shanxi. But all had one thing in common; they were on the Yellow River or one of its major tributaries. The river runs through Chinese history as a constant watery thread, uniting different rules down the centuries.

The Zhou dynasty (1122 BC–249 BC) established its seat in Shanxi at the long forgotten city of Hao, shifted downriver to Loh in Henan, and then once again downstream to Huali. It was a time of constant warfare and rivalry between feudal states which owed only lip service to the emperor, an age marked by treach-

ery, assassination, rebellion and upheaval. But as rulers and warriors struggled for supremacy, life for the peasants continued to be regulated more by the flow of the mighty river on whose banks they lived than by the histrionics of emperors, rival kings, contesting nobles and marauding barbarians.

The written language developed, cash was minted, irrigation improved, and in the town of Qufu in Shandong province a child was born in 551 BC who was to have an impact on his nation more lasting, more penetrating, than that of any ruler. Kang Jungni, whom we know as Confucius, grew up in poverty and spent his early life as a minor civil servant. He resigned because he refused to serve a government that expelled its legitimate lord. Taking to teaching, he swiftly drew idealistic disciples attracted by his philosophy of duty and loyalty. Confucius spent much of his adult life as a political exile from his home dukedom of Lu. Aged sixty-seven, he was permitted to return and complete work on his code of ethical principles. Pondering the ways of man, he worked to complete his lifetime task, the Annals of Lu or the Spring–Autumn Classics. The profound impact of his teachings on twenty-five centuries of Chinese civilisation cannot be underestimated. He laid the philosophical basis of family respect, filial duty and obedience which still in many respects guide hundreds of millions of Chinese in the conduct of their daily lives. After being posthumously disgraced by Red Guards in the Cultural Revolutionary hiatus, Confucius is now once again a prophet greatly honoured in his own country. His family cemetery where vandals smashed statues in the upheaval of the 1960s, has been restored and is open to the public; it is now the destination of organised tours for foreigners and Chinese alike.

As the Zhou dynasty faded, drowning in a sea of blood, the lands along the Yellow River collapsed into a welter of confused warfare and constant conflict. Alliances were forged and disintegrated. New bonds were struck between rival states, and armies marched across the land. The state of Chu warred with Tsi in 312 BC, and when defeated 80 000 of its soldiers were beheaded. Tsin's monarch fought with the kingdom of Han in 308 BC, and 60 000 soldiers of the vanquished army lost their heads. Tsin and Chu fought in 298 BC, and the executioners despatched 50 000 captive troops. As always, it was the peasants who suffered most in these endless upheavals during which rival lords vied for supremacy.

The Qin dynasty was born as bloody and lawless as the latter years of the Zhou. Warlords roamed the land, feudal rulers waged ceaseless warfare against neighbours, kings and princes feuded and plotted. From this chaos emerged a soldier named Wang Pan, himself the son of a famed general who had pacified powerful imperial foes.

Now known as Qinshihuang, the son soon proved himself a worthy and imaginative campaigner. He used the Huanghe itself as a weapon when laying seige to the city of Wei in 225 BC. The ruler of Wei, King Kia, stubbornly refused to surrender his capital. Rather than sending his troops to storm the imposing walls of

BRUNDAGE COLLECTION/LAURIE PLATT WINFREY INC

However abstruse their purpose or subtle their decoration, the underlying humour of much early Chinese art can be seen in this Shang *huo* figure, with a smiling animal head surmounting a vessel whose surface is elaborately figured.

Left
The importance of the Huanghe in Chinese history inspired not only great works of science and engineering, but rich developments in art. This hanging scroll from the Tang dynasty portrays a nobleman's palace built beside the broad and placid river.

The Ching-ming Festival on the River, by Chang Tse-Tuan, depicts life in and around the Song capital of Kaifeng. Under the reign of Emperor Shih-tsung, Kaifeng was the focal point of a web of waterways that embraced the Yangtze delta, the Shandong peninsula, the inland prefectures to the south and the seaports of Zhejiang. Chang Tse-Tuan's lively architectural style brings the everyday concerns of the twelfth century to vivid life, with details that can still be seen in today's China.

the city, Wang Pan ordered his men to lay down their swords and take up farm implements. They threw a dam out into the river, diverting the waters on to the plain and into the city of Wei. Swamped amid the rising waters, the enemy surrendered. Four years later, with other kingdoms either destroyed or paying tribute, Wang Pan consolidated his rule. He claimed the mantles of the three sovereigns and five emperors of antiquity, uniting their titles into one, Huang Ti (Royal Emperor.) It is under the name of Qinshihuang that he is remembered as the monarch who first unified China.

He was a political genius as well as a wily general. He ruled with a fist of iron; all who opposed him were put to death along with their families. As he clamped his law on the land, Qinshihuang tramped his domains up and down the Yellow River. On the peak of sacred Mount Tai he erected a memorial stone inscribed with his accomplishments. On other mountains in Shandong he raised other stones, but his most lasting memorial was the idea of one China, universal, as an indivisible state, a single entity, a distinct society. It is an idea which has never died, a philosophy adhered to today with equal fixation by Beijing and Taipei, both of which insist on the concept of One China.

METROPOLITAN MUSEUM OF ART

Qin rule did not long outlast the great unifier. Three years after his death, the Duke of Pei marched on the capital of Hien-yang, close by the river, and after four years of savage campaigning was proclaimed emperor of a new dynasty, the Han. Born of blood and turmoil, the Han was to go on to glory. From that time, the Chinese people have been known by the dynastic title, proud to call themselves Sons of Han. It was a time of swift expansion; the imperial boundaries stretched far from the Yellow River, up the Changjiang (Yangtze River) to Sichuan and down to Guangzhou (Canton). But the heart of the empire and its capital was in the old cultural heartland on the Huanghe.

There were disadvantages, to be sure. In addition to the floods which swept through palaces as surely as they swamped the humble homes of peasants, there were other perils of having the imperial city in the north. As China developed into a settled civilisation in which sophisticated agriculture formed a solid economic basis for prosperity, it became increasingly a target of envy and awe for the wild nomadic tribes which prowled outside the Great Wall. No wall, no matter how great, could stop the incursions. Emperors could dispatch millions of men to garrison the frontiers, but not even the gigantic population of China under the Tang

Presenting the Peach of Immortality, from the Yuan dynasty (1260–1368), shows the new awareness of the future that pervaded China during Mongol rule: a period followed by the consolidation and civilisation of the 300-year-long Ming dynasty.

(AD 618–907) could prevent constant raids and invasions. Once inside the Wall, barbarians plundered and killed, and the imperial capital, be it at Xi'an, Luoyang, Kaifeng or Beijing, was always within striking distance of invaders. The temptation to move south must have been great, especially when the Yangtze valley came firmly under Chinese rule and its rice-based agricultural economy began to dominate. But the attraction, which must have been very considerable, was always resisted. The political realities overrode other considerations, and the capital stayed firmly in the basin of the Yellow River. The notable exceptions are the brief sojourn of the Southern Song in Hangzhou from 1127 to 1279 when the Jurchen Tartars occupied the north and the even briefer period when Generalissimo Jiang Kaishek (Chiang Kai-shek) established his capital in Nanjing in the 1930s as Japanese invaders threatened the land. During such periods of uncertainty as the Warring States (500 BC–221 BC), the Three Kingdoms (AD 220–280) and the Five Dynasties (907–960) there were of course numerous minor capitals.

For as long as people have lived in the valley of the Huanghe, the prosperity of the societies along the river depended on its abundant waters, the fertility of the loess soil and the skill and toil of the peasants. For almost as long, this endless hard work to make the land bear fruit has resulted in a string of bizarre autocratic rulers who misused the wealth based on agriculture. Many of the rulers of ancient dynasties were sober, conscientious lords dedicated to improving the physical standard of living of their subjects and their mental well-being, to promulgate just laws and bring peace and order to the realm. Many others were wasteful and irresponsible spendthrifts whose lives were dedicated to debauchery and pleasure. Others were a combination of both. Even the Great Unifier, Qinshihuang, spent much of his life in a paranoid terror of assassins, and buried alive scholars with whose teachings he disagreed and ordered the mass executions of the populations of entire districts where he had been criticised.

Not all rulers were obsessed with politics and conquest. Indeed, many cared little for the burdens of office and were happy to leave the daily running of the land to bureaucrats as they attended to more personal matters, notably copious jugs of wine, large numbers of women and, occasionally, song.

The Emperor Yang of the Sui dynasty reigned at Xi'an and in the course of a lifetime devoted mainly to the earnest pursuit of pleasure had two million men working to build forty palaces. He liked boats and had a lake 5 kilometres wide built with three artificial islands 30 metres high raised in the middle. On this placid waterway filled from the River Wei, he sailed in pleasure vessels 65 metres long and four storeys high with all 120 cabins stocked with selected concubines. The shores of the lake were surrounded with villas also occupied by beauties should the emperor weary of life afloat. Ashore, he would ride in the moonlight accompanied by thousands of his concubines and courtesans across a park 50

FREER GALLERY/NEWSWEEK

*N*ot even the Tang dynasty's vitality could stop incursions by barbarians, and this painting of the eighth century Empress Yang Kuei-Fei mounting a horse is today an ironic comment on the inability of China's army to withstand the Mongol cavalry.

BRUNDAGE COLLECTION/LAURIE PLATT WINFREY INC

*A*s civilisation grew along the banks of the Huanghe, everyday items took on significance far removed from their humble origins. This bronze *chueh*, or ritual vessel, from the later Shang dynasty is descended from containers for heating wine.

kilometres wide. When the leaves fell in autumn, an army of retainers had to constantly decorate the trees with fresh vegetation to give the appearance of spring.

The sexual appetites of many of the rulers of China were prodigious. Life in court was often ruled by quarrelling armies of eunuchs who plotted and schemed with favoured concubines in endless conspiracies of the bedchambers. The politics of the harems were frequently more vicious and corrupt than those of the nation. Certainly, no quarter seems to have been given among the fight for supremacy of the ladies of the court as they struggled to find favour with the Son of Heaven. Yen Sz-ma, first emperor of the Western Jin, reigned at Luoyang. After the defeat of the kingdom of Wu in 280, he added 5000 women of Wu to his harem, already several thousands strong. The emperor liked to relax by driving through the considerable area of the ladies' quarters in a carriage drawn by goats. Where they stopped, he alighted and dallied. To tempt the goats to stop at their doors, cunning concubines laid down tasty bamboo leaves amid pools of salt water. Courtroom intrigue was no mere idle gossip but deadly serious warfare.

When Yen died, his son took the throne. The legendary rivalry between Chinese mother and daughter-in-law evidently existed in the royal family, because the new empress ordered the murder of the dowager's family. The mother-in-law stubbornly declined suicide so she was starved to death; the empress then demonstrated suitable filial piety by honouring the mother of her husband whom she had gone to such lengths to kill.

Court scandals proliferated throughout history; the scheming of the eunuchs in the last days of the Qing dynasty at the start of this century would not have seemed out of place 4000 years earlier. Annals recording the last stages of the Xia dynasty tell of the extravagant love affairs of the Emperor Kie Kuei in 1786 BC. He led an expedition against a rebellious local chieftain in Shanxi and as part of a peace settlement gained the chief's daughter, Mei Hi, as concubine. She swiftly won supremacy in the bedchamber. Besotted, the emperor 'built her a chamber of precious stones, ivory porticoes, marble terraces, jade bed, had luxurious music, a mountain of meat, a forest of dried meat, a lake of wine on which boats moved and 3000 people drank like cattle at the beating of a drum.'

Emperors did not have it all their own way. In 396, Emperor Hiao Wu, when drunk, told his favourite concubine, aged thirty, that she was too old. He dropped off into an intoxicated slumber and she suffocated him with a pillow. Eight centuries later, Emperor Kuang Tsung of the Southern Song admired the white hands of a palace woman. Next day the empress, known as a woman of strong temper, sent her lord a box containing the delicate hands he had so adored.

The deadly frivolity in the imperial courts and the often whimsical cruelty of the emperors was relieved by periods of rule by sagacious and benevolent leaders. Many are forgotten, others dimly remembered. One who brought peace to the

Overleaf

*I*n this river landscape, *A Market Village by the River*, dating from the Sung dynasty of the eleventh century, the river and its surrounding village are alive with the animated scenes of daily life.
NATIONAL PALACE MUSEUM, TAIWAN/AMERICAN HERITAGE

FREER GALLERY/LAURIE PLATT WINFREY INC

*F*ine bronzeware such as this twelfth century BC animal-inspired *kuang* or wine storage vessel, which has a duck's head and a monster mask on the tail, was typical of the Shang dynasty's artistic creativity and mastery of form and material.

realm and prosperity to its people was Tai Tsung of the Tang dynasty. He selected honest and fearless ministers and, untypically, paid heed to their advice. He sent home 3000 court ladies he had inherited. Tai Tsung had conquered the nation for his father, and when he himself sat on the Dragon Throne, one of his first acts was to dispatch thirteen officials as his eyes and ears to the countryside; a major task was to examine the dykes and embankments of the Huanghe and carry out repairs. Tai Tsung, unlike many other rulers, knew well where lay the basic strength of his realm. He appointed his ninth son as heir and cautioned the young man about the true value of the empire: 'If you know the toil of sowing and reaping, you will always have rice.' On a trip across the Yellow River, the wise ruler pointed out to his son certain similarities: 'The water carries a boat and upsets a boat. The people are as the river and the ruler as a boat.' Unfortunately, few emperors paid such care to the edification of their sons and the welfare of the people.

Left

Despite modernisations along the river, life on the Huanghe remains, for many, as it has been for centuries. Traditional vessels still ply the waterways.

A late eighteenth century *cloisonné* plaque depicts a Dragon Boat Festival, an event that began as a pagan attempt to placate angry river demons but one that soon took on all the lively enjoyment of a fair in China's river cities and towns.

BRUNDAGE COLLECTION/LAURIE PLATT WINFREY INC

黄河源

源頭

THE HEADWATERS

MONGOL LEGEND HAS it that after the Horde imposed its ferocious will on China its leaders dispatched a military expedition to the unknown reaches of the far western fringe of Han civilisation to probe the extent of the realm. Part of the charge to this adventure into the unknown was to find the source of the river that flowed through the area. When they did so, the soldiers erected a stone pillar at the head of a tiny stream and inscribed on the tablet the message that here lay the start of the river which watered the Chinese possessions of the Great Khan.

Five centuries later, explorers from another conquering power, the Manchus of the Qing dynasty, were dispatched on a similar mission. The Ch'ien Lung emperor, one of the greatest rulers in all of China's long history, had sent adventurers questing forth to find the source, there to pay homage to the god of the Yellow River. On their return the explorers told of a giant rock, 10 metres high, from which sprang crystal waters. The flow filled a pond on the rock, then cascaded to the high plateau of the frontier lands and trickled across the grasslands. Here, the explorers reported to the imperial court, was truly the start of the mighty stream that took life and prosperity to the plains.

Today, no trace remains of Mongol tablet or Manchu monolith. But fascination with the source of the Huanghe remains as intense as it has been since the dawn of Chinese history when the ancestors of the Han people scratched a living from the pale ochre soil along its banks. In every dynasty that soared, blossomed and

Macho Chuguo reads the sign in Tibetan script alongside the Chinese characters: 'Source of the most beautiful river in the world'. The horns of a long-dead yak mark the spot where the first tiny bubbles seep from the earth to begin the scientifically determined source of the Huanghe.

*L*ong deprived of modern medical aids, the remote Tibetan tribespeople now avail themselves of advice given by China's corps of famed barefoot doctors. Glasses for this old man would have been an unthinkable luxury a few years ago.

wilted along the course of the river over the fifty centuries of Chinese legend and history, people have wondered about what lay upstream. Ancient soothsayers told of a mystic stream that rose on the flanks of a sacred mountain in the remote Karakoram Ranges, flowed westward and dipped underground beneath the deserts of Xinjiang, then to spring to life and the surface again on the high Qinghai plateau. Other dynasties held other theories, and the Sui, the Tang, the Song all sent forth explorers into the barren loneliness of the highlands to seek the source.

This quest for the spot where the river rises continued under modern rule. In the past three decades, Chinese scientists, irrigation experts and flood-control cadres pushed upstream from the twin lakes of Gyaring and Ngoring once credited as the source to the slopes of 5442-metre Yagradagze Shan. Here, Chinese scientists have now determined, lies the true source of the Yellow River. The stream seeps out of a gentle slope on the northern flank of the 'Roof of the World'; the bubbling trickle of crystal water appears very different from the boiling, silt-laden flood that is the common image of the Yellow River. Hydrographers have for decades studied the upper reaches of the river, using special equipment to measure the power of the various tributary streams to check which one was the major source of the headwaters. These lengthy and exhaustive examinations helped select one flow from the hundreds that bubble out of the semifrozen ground and gradually meld together to form a stream.

It was to this modest brook trickling through ice banks past the skeleton of a yak that a documentary team from Chinese and Japanese television came in their search for the highest headwater of the Huanghe. They were led by men who best know the waterways that gather to form the birthplace of the freshets and creeks, officials of the River Source Research Party of the Yellow River Conservancy Commission. Here, they erected yet another tablet to mark the birthplace of the Yellow River. A few metres away from where the pure spring gushes from the sparse short marsh grass, they put up a tablet in Tibetan and Chinese marking the source of the Huanghe. In Tibetan the sign reads 'Machu Chuguo' – the source of the most beautiful river in the world.

At 4575 metres above sea-level, navigators from among the scientific team and television crew marked on their charts the exact spot where the water surfaced. At latitude 35°1′13″ N and longitude 95°59′24″ E, the river's birthplace is 2100 kilometres as the eagle flies from where it meets the Yellow Sea. But in its gigantic loops and turns the river covers 5464 kilometres before it runs into the Gulf of Bohai.

Irrigation and flood-control experts estimate that a drop of water bubbling from the spring on Yagradagze Shan would take a month to reach the estuary. To begin this tumbling journey through ice plateau and steppe and loess canyon and plain, the waters that will become the Yellow River flow across the austere landscape of Qinghai.

HIROYUKI USAMI

Wild rugged and beautiful, Anyemaqen Mountains spire above highland meadows. Seldom visited, this Swiss-like highland country is home to nomadic herdsmen whose flocks graze its slopes. Its jungle-clad lower reaches are inhabited by bears, deer and other game.

A Tibetan woman from the small town of Matau, high on the Qinghai plateau.

Right

*D*ressed in sheep-skinned splendour, hat raffishly aslant and clutching his rifle, this young Tibetan is on his way to temple at Darlag.

This is China's least-known province, a barren, treeless land of haunting beauty. Six times larger than Japan, nine times bigger than Britain, seventeen times the area of New York State, with an area of 720 000 square kilometres and a population of fewer than four million, Qinghai is one of the emptiest quarters of China. Even within this vast expanse, the ethnic mixture that makes up the population is scattered unevenly. Most live in the cultivated area in the east section of the province, around the capital of Xining or in other towns. Here the plateau dips, comparatively, to 2000 metres above sea-level and waters from the Yellow River, its tributaries and other waterways make settled farming possible. The people are a mixture: Tibetans, Mongols, Hui, Tu, Sala, Kazak and other national minorities make up about half the population.

But in the high lands in the centre of the province, where the winds never cease blowing and where great rivers are born, people are a rarity. The land is virtually uninhabited. The few hardy people who eke a living in this high, dry, cold land are tough Tibetan nomads whose homes are felt tents and whose belongings are all that can be loaded on to a packhorse. They follow their herds of cattle, yak and sheep over the empty grasslands. Centuries of folklore have shown the rovers that the land is not as barren as it first appears. Rare herbs are here, flowers and roots that can yield a handsome profit when sold to wandering herbalists.

How long these upland steppes will be left for the roamers of the Roof of the World is a matter of conjecture. As hydrographers ponder the river, geologists and metallurgists have been prowling the plains and mountains, chipping hammers and sample boxes in hand. Their finds have been impressive, and ominous for those who would like to see remote Qinghai preserved as a last unspoiled frontier. Lead, zinc, copper and chrome have been found in large quantities. So have potassium, nickel, iron, coal and gypsum, boron, asbestos and mirabilite. Oil deposits have been discovered beneath the inhospitable frozen surface. Chinese economists call the area 'treasure mountains' and industrialisation has begun.

But little of the development of the province can be seen around the upper reaches of the Yellow River. It remains desolate, remote, unpeopled. As the first brook spills down between clumps of stunted grass, it soon joins others to make a stream. A mere 30 centimetres wide, it weds itself to more tiny watercourses sliding across the plateau, gathering to its flow the waters that will make it mighty. First, however, it seems to lose its momentum on a wide plain where the infant waterway oozes into a maze of marshes. The bogs are treacherous, and the few who venture into these lonely uplands tread carefully here.

As the river emerges from the swamps, it flows clear and sparkling in the highland sun to form the twin lakes Ngoring and Gyaring. Places of desolate beauty, framed by the snowy Bayan Har mountains, the lakes adorn the plateau. People come here for different reasons: the Han to fish for the abundant, scaleless

YASUHIRO HAYASHI

*H*er kitchen a space on the floor of a draughty tent, a Qinghai herdswoman makes a meal from butter from her yak and millet flour, the tsamba meal that provides the staff of Tibetan life.

Previous pages

*I*n the brief summer of the highlands, wildflowers bloom on the Qinghai plateau where mountains are reflected in the placid waters of the lake known to wandering Tibetan herdsmen as the sea where stars dwell.

HIROYUKI USAMI

huangyu (yellow fish), and Tibetans, who hold the fish holy, to pray. Downriver is the first sign of human permanence, the tiny hamlet of Mato where a handful of Tibetans herd sheep.

Humans are rare here; in consequence nature flourishes. The lakes joined by the umbilical cord of the gathering Huanghe are a paradise for beast and bird. Hares, rabbits and marmots abound. Rare white-mouthed deer, tough and hardy despite their delicate appearance, are unique to this corner of the plateau. The elegant black-neck crane, too, can only be found here. Other visitors come from afar to breed in the still waters, like the huge India geese which every season flap their way over the Himalayas to lay their eggs and raise their young. Legends live on when the birds arrive; Buddhists believe that when the Tang dynasty Princess Wencheng was sent to Tibet to take religion to the fierce nomads and marry their king, the geese acted as messengers to carry news of her back to Xi'an. Gods reign still in these quiet rolling hills, many of which are topped with stupas. Here Tibetan pilgrims pray for safe passage over the snows to sacred Lhasa. The *obos*, as the cairns are known, lead the way to Lhasa, and on the long trek to pray at the holy city the faithful mark the stages of their journey by walking around the stupas thrice, telling their prayer beads, which contain the mystic number of 108 beads.

The river runs on, across the plains and sweeping by the foot of gentle hills. It is still 3000 metres above sea-level, but travellers who scratch the surface can find shells. The high plateau used to be ocean bed, but as the Himalayas were upthrust from the earth's crust, the growing mountains dragged with them the land that became the Tibetan–Qinghai plateau. More than 500 kilometres downriver from its source, the Huanghe makes its first important rendezvous with man. In most other parts of China, the town of Matau would be so tiny as to be insignificant. Here, where there is nothing else, the settlement of 1000 nomadic Koro Tibetan tribesmen is a veritable metropolis that stands out as starkly on maps as it does on the plains themselves, simply because there is nothing else.

Gathering volume from a thousand tributaries, the Huanghe also gathers speed and force as it drops down from the high plateau, falling 1000 metres by the time it skirts snow-clad Anyemaquen, yet another natural focal point once worshipped in the Tang dynasty as the font of the river. The moon is wooed by howling wolves, and in the forested slopes protected from the winds prowl bear and other game. Ceaselessly questing for the plains, the growing might of the river swirls east and south towards Sichuan until, blocked by mountains, it swings back on itself and heads north and west.

This is the first of the great nine curves the river will make on its tortured journey across northern China. The part of Sichuan touched briefly by the Yellow River is a forbidding place, far different from most of the huge inland basin that makes up China's most populous province. This fringe of Sichuan carries with it

YASUHIRO HAYASHI

*D*ancing into another age, Tibetan children take traditional steps across the high plateau during a rare nomad festival near Lake Gyaring.

dread legends of the modern age because it was through this nightmarish swamp of sodden ice, peat bogs and quicksand that Mao Zedong led the main forces of the Red Army on the most frightful stage of the entire 10 000 kilometres of the Long March. The toll was appalling. The revolutionary army tramped into the soggy plain 3500 metres above sea-level and found themselves in a dank world of watery horror. The plains of Songpan have more rain than any other part of the entire river course. The water has nowhere to run and lies atop stagnant beds of mud. Starving, eating grass to survive, tormented by swarms of mosquitos, the soldiers died by the thousands of exposure, starvation and exhaustion. Men and horses were sucked down into the bogs to disappear forever in the Sea of Death. Even today, the few survivors of the epic trek shudder as they remember the horrors of the marshlands. It was worse than the constant battles with pursuing Guomindang armies, they recall. More frightening than scaling the snowy mountains, as terrifying as swimming flooded rivers. The marshlands episode is etched in horror on the minds of a generation of Chinese.

Left
In a timeless composition, mounted Tibetan nomads near the town of Maqu in Gansu province survey their empty and eerily beautiful realm.

Slowly from this soggy, treacherous wasteland, the waters seep north to flow down streams into the river. After briefly flowing along 150 kilometres of Sichuan's border, the Huanghe does an unlikely complete about-face and heads back the way it came, northwest into Qinghai, before making yet another loop across the steppes towards the east.

WILLIAM NG

Dawn rises over the walled city of Xi'an, Shaanxi province.

眾多民族、眾多信仰

DIFFERENT PEOPLES, DIFFERENT BELIEFS

OVER THE PLAINS of the central plateau in Qinghai province echoes the low mournful lament of the *ragdune*. The 3.5 metre horn sends out a rolling, droning tone that reverberates off the hills and into the cloudless skies. There it attracts the attention of the ceaseless sentinels of the air, the vultures. First one bird wheels, drops from its patrolling pattern in the sky down towards the offering on earth. Kilometres away, another bird sees the downward spiral and swoops to follow. Soon the sky is full of vultures flapping to the feast. These ungainly, ugly creatures appear to be refugees from a prehistoric era. But to the devout monks who have summonsed them, they are the messengers of God, sent to bear to heaven the souls of the departed. Tibetans still consign their dead to the next world through the ancient rite of the platform. After relatives farewell their beloved, the corpse is laid out in the open and eaten by birds. It is a ceremony performed daily at the larger monasteries.

The vultures which patrol nearby skies know well what to expect. As the monks carry the body away from the temple, the birds have begun already to gather, flying in expectant circles through the clear air. The *ragdune* sounds dully, and a flute fashioned from a human thighbone, the *gandan*, pipes shrilly above the chorus of echoing *sutras* being chanted by assembled monks. Eagerly, the vultures hit the platform and feed off the corpse. Their task completed the bloated birds waddle into flight and flap their way back into the sky. With them, the monks believe, the messengers from heaven take the spirit of the deceased to God. Murderer or saint, horse robber or honest pilgrim, the dead are all equal and the vultures carry them to paradise.

*B*eneath the eves of the Taer Temple, a monk in traditional robes prepares to make a pilgrimage to a nearby hillside, where the Buddha's silken portrait will be revealed.

SEIGO OTSUKA

*M*onks at the Taer Temple believe this impression of a foot in the unpolished wood of the temple's floor was created when a particularly devout monk bent in prayer. It is regarded as one of the miracles of Qinghai Lamaism.

Right
The Paradise of Amitabha Buddha, an eighth-century scroll from Tun-huang, shows the Buddha and his acolytes beneath a *bodhi* tree, physically and symbolically removed from earthly concerns.

Previous pages
*H*orns, bells, gongs and chanted sutras hail the messengers of God when monks at the Charang Temple near Darlag carry out a traditional funeral. After laying out the body, the monks sit in prayer as their long brass horns echo through the valley. Soon the vultures arrive and devour the dead. Buddhists believe the birds carry the remains to heaven.
HIROYUKI USAMI

Although religion has been officially discouraged since the communist victory in China in 1949 and the Red Guards campaigned viciously against the faithful of all beliefs in the Cultural Revolution, Buddhism is still a vibrant, living way of life. It is more than just a faith; part of the fabric of being for the Tibetans of the upper river. The 1960s drive against religion was just one of countless persecutions. In 574, to give but one example, Emperor Wu of the Chou kingdom fixed religions in order of precedence – Confucianism, Taoism, Buddhism – then banned the latter two, razed their temples, burned their scriptures and forced their religious to return to secular life. In the Boxer Rebellion, converts to Christianity and missionaries were slaughtered up and down the length of the river with the enthusiastic connivance of Qixi, the Empress Dowager.

Although Tibetans have been ardent and devout Buddhists for the past 1200 years and the outward trappings of their faith are everywhere apparent, they still cling to older beliefs based on the teachings of tribal shamans. In many parts of the high country, they worship still the spirits of nature, hold fast to a fear of demons, believe that in each blade of grass on the steppes a god dwells. But it is their form of Buddhism, which many claim to be the most closely linked to the original Indian version, that dominates their daily lives. Universally, the Tibetans pray for a return from his self-exile of the god-king, the Dalai Lama. He chose to flee over the Himalayas to India at the time of the Chinese invasion of Tibet in 1959. His people want him to return.

The signs of Buddhism are everywhere through the swathe of Qinghai, Sichuan and Gansu where the river runs. This was once part of Amdo, a Tibetan empire. Their rule has long gone, but the people remain. Even where there are no people to be seen, the wide horizons empty as the nomads take their herds to far-off pastures, the *obos* dot the hillsides and the prayer flags flap their messages in the endless winds. They can hear the word of God, the Tibetans say, in the ceaseless crackling of the white flags whose inscriptions are kept alive by the eternal winds.

The daily lives of the Tibetans are guided by faith and superstition. So are those of their Mongol neighbours along the upper reaches of the river. In addition to the strictures and disciplines of Lamaist Buddhism, the Mongols have inherited other beliefs from their turbulent ancestors: a guest takes care never to whistle in a yurt, and it is good form to leave your horsewhip outside the door.

The horse is to the people of the high plains more than an animal. Like their religion, it is a vital part of their way of life. The Mongol armies of Genghis Khan and his descendants were known as the Devil's Horsemen, with good reason. It was their stocky, hardy horses that propelled them astonishingly over a continent and a half from the high steppes to the gates of Vienna. Horsemanship remains a virtue, a claim to manliness, for both peoples. The greatest honour a Tibetan nomad can imagine is to breed a magnificent steed and race it faster than any other

HIROYUKI USAMI

*F*rom the Charang Temple wall, near Darlag, the Buddha and his acolytes bestow blessings on passers-by.

horseman of the plains. This is constantly tested at impromptu race meetings held throughout the short highland summer. Fuelled by barley beer, the sportsmen gather with their mounts. Standing in the stirrups, they give cries to ancient gods that the races are about to begin, then whip their steeds into a gallop over the plains. Into the air go hundreds of pieces of paper with pleas for victory printed on them. With the beer and the good humour and the ground littered with paper like discarded betting tickets at a race course in the western world, the race meetings of the high plains have a festive feeling. But in times past there was a more serious aspect to these gatherings; young boys were there to prove their manhood, and the men were there to show they were ready for war. Though the motives these days are different the horsemen still whip their lathered steeds across the high plains.

Here is Tibetan land, stark and lonely, as it has been for centuries. Their ancestors rode on Qinghai's plains as fierce warriors before the Princess Wencheng of the Tang dynasty arrived with her coterie of handmaidens and servants. The princess was to wed King Sontsengampo of the Tibetans. She and her escort had travelled for months up the Yellow River from the court of her father, the emperor, in distant Xi'an. The king came to meet his bride on the shores of the linked lakes of Gyaring and Ngoring. Both believed the Yellow River was born where the clean mountain waters left the lakes to begin the journey down to the far plains. Princess Wencheng took with her more than her dowry. She also carried the Buddhist religion. The standard modern view of Tibetans is of a gentle people living a devout and peaceful life in icy meadows. It was not always so. At the time of the Tang, the Tibetans were a nation on horseback, savage fighters as fierce as the Mongols but without the ruthless and efficient brutality that the Khans were to display when they butchered their way to domination four centuries later. Did the message of Buddhism carried by Princess Wencheng bring peaceful enlightenment to the wild horsemen of the highlands? Some scholars think so.

The religion also brought medicine to the high country. Monks have traditionally been healers of the body as well as pacifiers of the soul. These days, China's huge corps of barefoot doctors, frontline troops of the medical profession who take basic cures and hygiene to the remotest corners of the land, regularly tend to isolated communities of wanderers on lonely Qinghai steppes. Among them are a number of paramedics trained in the unique form of Tibetan traditional healing, a discipline that leans heavily on traditional self-reliance. The Tibetans of the past had only herbs and magic to cure themselves from all ailments. Medicines and methods used today by traditional doctors tend broadly to follow old precepts. The herbs are as exotic as their names, things like 'winter worm, summer herb' which is an underground fungus that grows on buried larvae of worms. It is held to be a powerful cure. So are potions made from rabbit's heart, gallbladder of a cow, selected roots, ground gems and deer horns. Shells found in the earth 4000 metres

HIROYUKI USAMI

*F*ree as the wind and as fast, Tibetan horsemen spur on their ponies as, banners aloft, they race across the Sichuan plains.

An elderly Tibetan seeks a professional opinion from a Buddhist monk skilled in traditional Tibetan medicine.

SEIGO OTSUKA

TSUGUSATO OMURA

Descended from the dreaded horsemen of the Khan, Mongols today are people of peace. Many, like these aged monks, have devoted their lives to the Buddha.

above the sea and fossil remains are, when finely powdered, also well regarded as cures for diverse ailments. Some of the medical lore handed down to modern Tibetans came from Indian Buddhist monks. More is based on the yin–yang balance of Chinese herbal medicine. A form of acupuncture using burning stubs helps cure internal ills diagnosed by Tibetan doctors, who use six fingers to feel simultaneous pulses in the patient's body.

As the river drops in altitude, the people change. Races of different ethnic groups live together. In ages past, they were often warring enemies, hated foes or feuding neighbours. These days, they are more likely to live in peace. Intermarriage is increasingly common. Tibetans, Turkic tribesmen, Han, Mongols, Manchu and Hui live in harmony on different stretches of the Huanghe. Buddhism, Islam, Confucianism, Taoism and Christianity all have their believers. There are even the Jews of Kaifeng (Henan province), the handful of remnants of one of the most remarkable communities ever to pass along the Silk Road and settle on the Yellow River. Once a proud and prosperous community of traders and craftsmen, they numbered several hundred at the time of the Yuan dynasty. They have since dwindled and are now but a curiosity for tourists.

TSUGUSATO OMURA

Where the lances of warriors and the banners of Mongol cavalry once dominated the skyline, the rooftops of Batou now feature that universal trademark of the twentieth century — the television aerial.

*T*rusty as a modern computer according to those skilled in its use, the abacus has long been an inextricable part of Chinese commerce. This receptionist totes up the number of visitors going to a Taoist temple.

Right
*T*he thin music of a mouth organ floats over the Huanghe as a budding musician from Ledu practises in solitude.

According to Taoist belief, China was born of the Huanghe. In mythology, the river flowed from the veins of the first man, Pan Ku. His head became a mountain, one eye the sun and the other the moon. Taoist priests can pinpoint the date; 961 962 210 BC is the most ancient given. During the period before humans ruined the land, Taoists hold, the entire length of the lands along the river from the Kunlun Mountains to the Yellow Sea was clothed in luxuriant forests. It was the Land of the Flowery Kingdom. Tame animals and friendly birds lived on abundant berries and nuts. The ground was carpeted with wildflowers, and the waters of the Huanghe were clean and clear. Life was easy and happy for the lucky people who lived on the river. Then came civilisation, and this happy state of affairs came to an end. Humans cut down the trees, lit fires among the forests, burned down the Flowery Kingdom. The rich ash of the fires fertilised the ground, and at first man the farmer was delighted with his crops. But then came the rain, the topsoil washed away, the river was polluted and discoloured. Clogged with mud and silt, it rose in flood. The Taoist parable of the Flowery Kingdom and the fall from grace and contentment of the people along the Huanghe parallels the story of Adam and Eve and the Garden of Eden.

The river joins communities together and it keeps them apart. For stretches reaching hundreds of kilometres there are no bridges, few ferries. It is often a matter of do-it-yourself or stay on your side of the river. Generations of practice have made perfect for horsemen on the upper river. They simply dismount on one side, take off their clothes and put them into a waterproof bag, then urge their mount into the water. Man and animal are an aquatic team; the horse swims powerfully into the rushing waters with the rider – now swimmer – clutching the tail with one hand and bag of possessions in the other. The current helps, swinging the travellers downstream. Striking for the distant shore the horse eventually ends up far downriver, but on the other side. The rider dresses, springs back on his mount and rides off. Tibetans crossing the river give a weird piercing cry that echoes from the cliffs. This is not an appeal for help but aimed at scaring off the fanged monster *Tsaru*, the dreaded legendary creature which inhabits the upper reaches and whose tooth-encrusted body slays intruders.

For those less adventurous, without a horse or who wish to avoid tempting *Tsaru*, there are ways to cross the river without getting wet. The most common is on a *yangpi* raft, a frail-looking vessel made of a few flimsy sticks laid atop inflated sheepskins. It appears a hazardous way to travel, but for hundreds of kilometres in Qinghai and Gansu there is no alternative way across the Huanghe. Even in Qinghai province the river is already 200 metres wide and running strongly, and for 300 kilometres from Matau to Dahli there is no bridge. With easy skill, sheepskins are turned fleece-side in, sewn and sealed, oiled and tanned, then blown up by mouth. With a framework lashed on top, the craft is put on the water; men,

*T*emple doors decorated with the visage of an angry guardian of the Path of Truth open to reveal an image of the Buddhist reformist teacher Tsuonkapa (1357–1419), founder of the *Gelupa* or yellow hat sect of which the Dalai Lama is the head.

women and children pile on, leaving yaks, cattle and horses held by reins and ropes to swim alongside. After paying a few *fen* the passengers on such makeshift ferries are taken across the river at hundreds of crossings. Despite appearing dangerous and although the *yangpi* services continue when the river is in full flood, there are few accidents reported.

Throughout the course of the Huanghe, legend, folklore, rumour and religion have blended over the centuries with historical fact. Up the Hei tributary in arid northern Gansu, the river bisects the most westerly section of the Great Wall and both rendezvous with the Silk Road. There in Jiuquan (Wine Spring) county is the Hexi Corridor, a vital pass into China. The Han dynasty was keenly awake to the significance of the pass and its use to enemies, and garrisons stood watch to prevent incursions.

One warrior who made good use of the natural protection of the pass was General Huo Qubang. In 121 BC he cunningly deployed his men and lured into a trap an enemy army intent on plunder. After a fierce battle, the intruders were destroyed and fled. So delighted with the victory was Emperor Wu Di that when he received news of the victory in far-off Xi'an he swiftly ordered a messenger to speed ten bottles of wine from the imperial cellars to his conquering soldiers. Legend holds that General Huo felt there was not enough wine to serve all the men who had fought and won with him. Instead of reserving the wine for the officers, Huo poured it into a nearby spring. The gods were impressed by such unaccustomed devotion of a general to his troops, and miraculously the water gushing from the spring turned into wine. The troops promptly went on a drinking spree. Although the wine issuing from the rocky earth of Jiuquan has long since turned back into water, the name of the county recalls that ancient battle.

So does one of the local industries, the manufacture of wine cups carved from blocks of jade quarried from the Qilian Mountains. The glasses are so thin they are translucent, and when filled with grape wine, the green, yellow or white jade cups are said to glow in the moonlight. According to the Tang poet Wang Han the greatest pleasure a drinker could have was to sip out of a Jiuquan jade. 'Delicious grape wine in a luminous cup,' he wrote.

Any culinary tradition depends basically on the climate and geography of the land where it originates. So it is along the Huanghe. The food of the nomads of the high steppes is significantly different from the diet of the lowland farmers. With modern transport and Han settlement of the Qinghai plateau and with scientific farming methods and industrialisation bringing some relief to the horrific legendary poverty in Gansu province, times are changing. But regional dietary patterns still hold true to a surprising extent.

The most basic of these is the consumption of grain. Broadly speaking, southern China eats rice, and the north consumes wheat. While this culinary truism is

TSUGUSATO OMURA

A train roars over one of the arched bridges that cross the Huanghe at Lanzhou. A communications and industrial centre, the city's two million people take pride in a long history that once saw Lanzhou the western Chinese hub of the Silk Road.

Pages 71–73

Four times a year, monks of the Yellow Hat sect climb the slopes near their famed temple to proclaim their faith and display a gigantic picture of the Buddha embroidered 250 years ago on silk. The pilgrimage up the hillside is made at New Year, in spring, summer and autumn; it is a colourful ceremony in which horns blare and the hills echo with the chants of sutras.
SEIGO OTSUKA

Fragile watercraft on the placid upper reaches of the Huanghe.

more or less correct, things along the Yellow River are made more complex by the changing altitude of the landscape. There are three tiers, a series of immense steps. First, there is the high country of the Gansu corridor and the Qinghai plateau. Then comes a huge step down to the loess plateau, the middle course of the river. Finally, there is a big step down to the enormous lowland flats of the North China Plain, watered by the Huanghe, its tributaries and other, lesser, streams and rivers. Speaking broadly, the food gets more sophisticated as the traveller goes downstream. From rude but hearty meals in nomad tents the scale of culinary achievement grows to the pinnacle of the classical cuisine of North China as one enters the open plains. The food of the highlands is staple: meat from their herds and hardy grain like millet or barley. The few vegetables that can be grown or herbs that can be gathered in the brief summer bring some welcome variety. Mutton and barley; the way of life as well as the diet is similar to that of Scottish crofters.

The basic staff of life is *tsamba*. It is, above all, an efficient food and well suited to the nomadic way of life. When ground and ready to eat, the roasted barley grain looks like fine sawdust from a light pine tree. Probably the best description of the staple food of Qinghai, Mongolia and much of the rest of northwest China was

SEIGO OTSUKA

HIROYUKI USAMI

With a cheerful smile, a shopkeeper in the Gansu town of Linxia invites visitors to taste his wares.

given by the noted traveller, writer and explorer Peter Fleming who went by horseback from Lanzhou to what is now Pakistan in the 1930s. On his seven-month journey he survived on *tsamba,* and at the end of the long trail vowed he would one day write an ode to the substance.

> You eat it in tea, with butter if you have got butter, or with mutton fat if you haven't got butter, or with neither if you have neither. You fill your shallow wooden bowl with tea, then you let the butter melt in the tea (the butter is usually rancid and has a good cheesy flavour); then you put a handful of *tsamba* in. At first it floats; then, like a child's castle of sand, its foundations begin to be eaten by the liquid. You coax it with your fingers until it is more or less saturated and has become a paste; this you knead until you have a kind of doughy cake in your hand and the wooden bowl is empty and clean. Breakfast is ready.

Such a simple repast is the daily fare of many in the high country. It is cheap, it is highly digestible, it is simple to prepare and carry (an important consideration when your home is a tent pitched every night where the herds have stopped), and it is sustaining. The diner can vary the taste at will from sweet to savoury by adding honey or pepper or chilies or whatever comes to hand. 'I would not go so far as to say that you never get tired of *tsamba,*' Fleming wrote appreciatively. 'But you would get tired of anything else much quicker.'

Just as food differs as the river descends, so does housing. In Qinghai, home to the herdsmen is a tent made of felt. Romantic, yes. Comfortable, hardly. Tents also house Mongol herdsmen in their homeland. But in the great industrial cities along the waterway from Lanzhou down to Jinan, big apartment complexes, forbidding rather than attractive, provide homes for the bustling urban workforces. It is in the countryside where the greatest change is to be seen. Since new economic thinking allowed peasants to work for themselves, there has been a quiet but significant financial revolution in the villages of China. It began in 1978 when the hated commune system was replaced by the 'responsibility' method of work under which those who work hard get more money. The result has been to create '10 000 yuan' families, mostly farm folk who make this incredible, for China, amount a year. Much of the money is spent on housing. Old mud huts are torn down, left to collapse or used to house animals as substantial new brick buildings rise alongside them. In some areas, more than half the population have built new homes for themselves in the past decade.

As the Yellow River surges into Gansu it carries already sufficient loads of saffron-hued silt to justify its name. But before it departs from Qinghai the river goes through one of the most dramatic transformations of its entire course, the breathtaking plunge through the gorge at Longyang. Here the cliffs have stubbornly refused to yield to the pounding waters, and the river is confined to a channel only 10 metres wide. According to local folklore, a fox can clear the river here

HIROYUKI USAMI

*M*uslims gather for a feast in the Hui Autonomous Region. Many Huis are indistinguishable from Han, but a sizeable percentage show traces of differing racial groups, harking back to forebears who came down the Silk Road or who journeyed with their herds from Central Asian pastures.

A traditional means of crossing upper reaches of the river has for many centuries been on *yangpi* rafts, frail frameworks of wooden poles lashed to inflated oiled sheepskins. Even in full flood, the light vessels bob across the turbulent waters.

Right

*G*azing out from a cave hewn from weathered seams of rock, Lord Buddha surveys the river at Binglingsi in the Liuchiaxia Gorge.

in one precarious leap from the lip of one cliff to scramble on to the precipice on the other side. Far below, the waters rage, boiling through the narrows as though propelled from a turbine. The full, awesome power of nature churns violently through the Longyang Gorge at the rate of seven tumultuous metres a second. Those few adventurers who choose to shoot these rapids, as did the documentary makers with their heavy television gear, usually do so on vessels of a traditional cast, the light *yangpi* rafts, inflated sheepskins tied together on wooden frames. The churning waves and whirlpools created by the wild currents toss the skin-and-air rafts along over the surface of the water, skipping like dragonflies rather than floating like ducks. It is a turbulent journey, the sky only a thin gash high above the water, the current madly crashing back from the unforgiving walls of granite. The battle between rock and water has been going on for tens of thousands of years. It is a war with no winners.

Flowing through Gansu, the river is more placid. Along the banks and up its many tributaries figures of Lord Buddha are carved in rock, and in the cave temples his likeness is repeated endlessly, 7000 times alone in the 194 caves that make up the holy places at Maijishan. Gansu is a meeting place of faiths, just as it is a gathering place for great tributaries to flow into the Yellow River. Buddhism lives among the Tibetans and Mongols. Islam is stamped firmly into the consciousness of the Hui, themselves a racial mixture of Han Chinese and the migratory waves from Central Asia that flowed along the Silk Road. Traders tramped these river banks – Marco Polo passed this way – to take the treasures of Cathay to Europe.

Within today's borders, the provincial capital of Lanzhou is in the geographical centre of China. But for centuries as power ebbed and flowed it was a frontier town on the fringe of empire, a garrison from which military commanders looked out anxiously towards the wild tribesmen of the Qinghai highlands and the turbulent, warring peoples of the steppes of Xinjiang. Restive Muslims rebelled in Gansu in the 1860s, and Imperial troops put down the uprising with appalling brutality in a war of retribution that lasted sixteen years. The Yellow River is said to have run red.

The Huanghe cuts across the narrowest section of the dumbbell-shaped province, an area of China spoken of with wonder for its awesome poverty. Even today, beggars are not uncommon; much of the 450 000 square kilometres of the province is desert or sparse steppe. Most of the people, including almost all the third of the population who are Uygur, Tibetan, Dongxian, Mongol or Hui, live in rural areas. The Han dominate the towns, including Lanzhou, bustling hometown for new emigrant Chinese brought in from throughout the nation as a workforce for the smoky chemical, machinery and metal factories.

Further along the river the great feat of nature meets one of the most imposing works of man, for it is in Gansu that Yellow River crosses Great Wall. The river

China's leading chemical centre, Lanzhou is a metropolis where modern technology not only provides jobs but attracts scientific and academic advances. Once a frontier town, Lanzhou is now one of the nation's major industrial cities.

formed a highway which brought barbarians from the west; the Wall was built to stop them. In the arid north of Gansu, ramparts of ancient forts preserved by the dry desert air still stand guard in lonely passes against barbarian intruders.

Chapters of China's ancient past are evident here where Buddhas carved from the rock stare impassively out over river and tributaries. In the Bingling Cave Temple at Liu Jia Gorge, some of the finest religious artistry in the country is proudly displayed by monks who guide visitors through the 195 grottoes where 694 stone Buddhas and eighty-two superb clay sculptures stare as impassively at camera-toting Americans as they once did on the young Marco Polo.

The gorge is also site of an impressive hydroelectric station, one of the biggest in China with capacity of 1225 million kilowatts. Economic planners claim proudly that they trapped the river in the gorge behind a huge dam, then put it to work. Every year, the hydroelectric turbines produce 5.7 billion kilowatt hours of power which, staff are quick to point out, is more than all of China in the bad old days before Liberation. Much of this power lights the impressive pollution of the industrial city of Lanzhou, now a major centre and a vital link in the overall national economic plan.

It is just past Lanzhou that the course turns north and the Huanghe begins the greatest of its nine bends, the huge curve that takes it north through Gansu, into the Muslim region of Ningxia, in a tremendous loop through the Mongol grasslands and then back southwards once again where it forms the borders of Shaanxi and Shanxi. Ningxia's 60 000 square kilometres have been given over since 1958 to an autonomous homeland for the nation's Muslims, or Hui people. Living amid Mongols, Manchus, Tibetans and Han in their own province, the Hui form 40 per cent of the population. They are themselves a racial mixture of diverse strains, many being indistinguishable, apart from their religion, from the Han Chinese.

It was in this corner of the Huanghe that the great conquerer Genghis Khan is said to have met his unseemly end. The man who brought terror to the world and much of it to subjugation came to his end not on the battlefield but in bed. Details of the legend differ, but in all versions the savage warrior is said to have become enamoured of a Tangut princess of outstanding beauty. He forced her husband to give the woman up, but when she was taken to the eager Khan the princess from out of her wardrobe produced a sharp hunting knife and castrated the man who was the scourge of the world. She escaped from his camp at Yinchuan, now the capital of the Islamic homeland, hurled herself in the Yellow River and drowned. Hence the Mongol name for the River of the Princess. (More prosaically, other historians hold that Genghis Khan died of internal injuries after being thrown from his horse during his campaign against the Tanguts.)

If the Yellow River is likened to a dragon, as it has been through antiquity, then this is the back of the crouching beast. By the time it leaves Gansu it is a beast

TSUGUSATO OMURA

*I*n the early morning half-light, the people of Baotou ride to work. Baotou, the iron and steel centre of Inner Mongolia, is one of the five major industrial suppliers in China.

衆生處代如電光
須臾業盡即无常
慈悲觀音濟群品
愛何波中作橋梁
捨施淨財成真像
光明曜晓綵繪莊
惟願亡者生淨土
三途免苦上天堂
時天復拾載庚午歳七月十五日畢功記
供養
弟子織染中監張有成一心

carrying an immense burden, one of silt. The waters are laden with a heavy suspended content of earth, and every metre the river runs it collects more.

Within the 'Great Bend' lies the Ordos, a swathe of desert and dry steppe. Over these plains galloped Mongol warriors, the Devil's Horsemen, before they burst out to conquer the world. Scholars believe the expression 'Horde' is a corruption of Ordos. The descendants of Genghis Khan remain there today. On a tributary is the capital of the Inner Mongolian Autonomous Region, Huhhot. In Mongol,the name means 'Green Town', and as everywhere in this dry and thirsty land the presence of reliable water means a bursting spread of emerald showing where irrigation allows crops to flourish. It does not happen frequently in this 1.2 million square kilometre province which spreads in a vast crescent over the northern border of China. The Yellow River encompasses a sizeable swathe of Mongolian land before it reaches the top of the Great Bend and swings east, then south into the loess lands of China proper.

Left

A portrait in silk of one of the Buddha's greatest Chinese followers, Bodhisattva Kuan-Yin, accepting offerings of love and respect shows the influence of traditional Chinese religious art in his fluid pose and costume.

Bringing technology to the aid of ancient tradition, wandering monks camp in nylon tents on the Songpan Plain in Sichuan.

浩瀚中游

THE MIDDLE REACHES

DOWN THE 700 kilometres of the Chinshen Valley where the Huanghe slashes between the ancient provinces of Shaanxi and Shanxi, tumbling and sliding through a valley shaped like a huge axe wound, more than a hundred major tributaries add their water and mud to its flow. These are lands old both geographically and historically. Nature has sculpted the course of the river for an estimated two million years. It cuts deeply into the loess plateau, and as the smaller siblings meet the mother stream they dump a billion tonnes of mud every year. From the air, the land looks like a tortured body. It is ravaged, scarred, clawed by erosion. Cancerous growths of rivers cut ceaselessly into the soft hills, forming gullies and ravines from which every downpour scours more earth. In ancient times, farmers prayed as they saw their lands disappearing. These days, scientists help them to plant drought-resistant trees and shrubs to fight erosion. It is here that the river gets its two major tributaries. From Gansu, the Wei rolls across Shaanxi, past towns already venerable before the founding of Rome. From the other side of the high country comes the Feng, storming down through Shanxi.

Up the Wei is the proud old capital of Xi'an and down to the southeast of its great walls is the sleepy farming valley of Lantian. It looks like any one of a thousand villages that sit dozing in the hot summers of the North China hills. But 850 000 years ago, Lantian had a very different aspect. Indeed, say ethnologists and anthropologists, in those distant times Shaanxi was a hot, steamy land, its jungles prowled by elephants, rhinoceros, sabre-toothed tigers and other fearsome creatures. And by an early ancestor of modern humans. In 1963, commune

Puffing homegrown tobacco on homemade pipes, these two venerable elders in Shaanxi relax after a day in the fields.

Shy smiles welcome visitors passing curious youngsters peering through a sliding wall panel on a Shaanxi home.

workers digging into a slope found some fossilised bones. The discovery caused intense excitement among scientists who dated the remains at about 850 000 years old. The thick cranial and jaw bones gave vital clues that helped them build up a portrait of what this early inhabitant of the Huanghe may have looked like. In a pavilion marked by upturned eaves and set amid an arbour, visitors can now rest in the shade and look at the hill where Lantian Man, our oldest known predecessor, walked upright more than 8000 centuries ago. It is impossible to conjure his thoughts, his way of life.

With later inhabitants, we are luckier. Thanks to the rich legacy they left behind, we know very well what manner of men and women occupied the same area 5000 years ago. They were no longer roamers but settlers. Not hunters nor nomads, but tillers of the rich yellow soil, growers of millet and barley, weavers, dyers, sculptors and moulders of clay. One of these earliest villages, occupied in the New Stone Age long before the mistiest dynasty began, has been found and excavated near the suburb of Banpo on the fringes of Xi'an. Small houses of mud built around a tiny courtyard and storage cellars contain scraps of pottery and early tools. A deep moat shows us that the inhabitants, whoever they may have been, were aware of a hostile world outside their walls. Shaanxi and its neighbouring province of Henan both lay claim to being the true cradle of the Chinese race. It is an argument that will never be resolved, one in which both sides have powerful points to make. Few of these arguments can weigh as much as the presence of the fabulous city of Xi'an, a metropolis at the time of Christ, a wonder still today.

Modern Xi'an, and Shaanxi, and the Yellow River valley and, to a large extent, China, are dominated today by a man who lived twenty-two centuries ago. The discovery of the tomb of Qinshihuang and his terracotta guardians was a magnet that attracted attention not only to the man but also to the empire he made, the people he ruled, the land he conquered, the river he sought so earnestly to control. The discovery of his tomb focuses the attention of the world not only on his reign but also on those that followed and the ones that went before.

In more ways than one does the historic core of the Yellow River exert a commanding and emotional tug on the heart of modern China. Xi'an, the magnificent city of legend on the Wei River, was for more than 1100 years capital of succeeding dynasties. The Great Unifier, Qinshihuang, held his court here after he welded the tribes and kingdoms and dukedoms of the Huanghe into the first Chinese empire. Without him, many scholars believe, China could have developed into a society like Europe, splintered, separate, diverse, rather than into the cohesive, universal civilisation it became. And in Xi'an, then known as Chang'an, ruled much of the glorious Tang dynasty, perhaps one of the greatest, a realm that saw brilliant flowering of pottery, painting and poetry and enormous strides in science and medicine. Marco Polo marvelled at Xi'an and many of the fables that spread

SEIGO OTSUKA

*A*bove ancient Xi'an, a pagoda crowns a hill.

YASUHIRO HAYASHI

*F*rom this humble room hacked out of the loess cliffs of Yanan, Mao Zedong led the communist revolution for more than a decade. Resting in this remote river market town after the rigours of the Long March, Mao and his lieutenants set up their headquarters in traditional cave houses. In Yanan they planned the Red Army campaigns against Japanese invaders and then oversaw the civil war that saw the People's Liberation Army march south to occupy the nation.

through Europe of the immense splendours of Cathay could be traced back along the route of travellers whose journeys took them to this terminal on the Silk Road.

The Western Zhou ruled here 1000 years before the start of the Christian era. In Xi'an, too, was the court of Qin and Sui, Han and Wei. No fewer than eleven dynasties counted the great city on the River Wei as their capital, and from far earlier times, in the long unwritten ages of the Shang, kings wielded power from here that spread far down the Yellow River and up into the loess highlands.

Outside Xi'an, among the many tombs identified but still to be carefully inspected, is that of Empress Wu Zetian. Concubine to one Tang emperor, wife to another, murderer of a third, she schemed and connived and butchered her way to power to rule in her own right, feared by the entire nation – with great justification – for almost half a century. She was as cruel as she was beautiful, as skilful as she was ruthless, a ruler who used torture as a routine instrument of policy. But despite her vile methods, or possibly because of them, her rule was efficient. The Empress Wu of Tang is compared with the Empress Dowager Qixi of the Qing and the fallen idol Jiang Qing, wife to the modern emperor, Mao Zedong. All three, separated by thirteen centuries, used powerful husbands so they themselves could grab the reins of control. All three are blamed for massacre, excesses and oppression. All three came from provinces watered by the river, reared by its legends.

SEIGO OTSUKA

*H*ot red peppers add piquancy to the dishes of Shaanxi and Shanxi, as well as a flash of colour to the drab ochre walls of cave homes. Chili and garlic are favoured condiments in many local dishes, giving spice to the plentiful vegetables grown on irrigated fields.

The tombs of Shaanxi are in many cases veritable cities of the dead; clustered around the burial place of a monarch are likely to be the graves of servants and courtiers and soldiers who, when their own time came, asked to be buried near the ruler they served. Archaeologists and other scholars from all over the world have been observers at excavations.

But Shaanxi also commands attention from scholars of more modern times. It was into the unremarkable small market town of Yanan, a drab, inhospitable, inaccessible settlement, that in 1936 tramped a procession of weary peasant soldiers. These were troops of the Red Peasants' and Workers' Army, and at their head was a disgruntled intellectual named Mao Zedong. It was the end of the Long March, and it was to Yanan that Mao had led those few of his men who survived with him and tramped and fought their way across China. If Xi'an and other ancient capitals along the Huanghe and its tributaries are places of pilgrimage for those curious about the imperial past, then Yanan is likewise a magnet for those wishing to visit the cradle of the New China. Here, hacked into the loess cliff face, is the cave home where Mao lived for most of the eleven years that Yanan was headquarters of the communists. Nearby are similar modest cave homes once occupied by other Red leaders like Zhou Enlai and Zhu De. Museums of the revolutionary period recall the modern legend of the Long March, but the more lasting legacy of communist rule can probably be seen in the heroic afforestation on the banks of the Yan River and the mighty construction works along the dykes downstream. Like emperors

*H*alf a century after the Long March passed through her home village, an old lady lies under her padded down cover for warmth and remembers the Red Army marching by, bringing a new era to China.

of old, Mao took seriously the strictures that warned that conquest of the river was vital for political control of the country.

But before the battle with the river could be joined, Mao and his followers had more immediate foes. He had headed to the poor, arid, backward north from the comparatively wealthy and lush south for two reasons, to escape the tightening clutches of Guomindang armies determined to exterminate 'Red bandits' and to confront the invading Japanese who had already snatched Manchuria from China. The communists preached that 'Chinese should not fight Chinese' and urged a united front of nationalist, communist and warlord armies to confront the Japanese and throw them out of China. Then a free China could try to solve its own problems in its own way.

This message was keenly received by many, including a brilliant general usurped from his native Manchuria by the Japanese. His name was Zhang Xueliang. His father, killed by Japanese agents in the fighting in Manchuria, was the 'Old Marshal' Zhang Tso-lin. So his son was known as the Young Marshal. But the communists' message of fraternity did not sit well with the Guomindang leader, Generalissimo Jiang Kaishek. In December 1936 he flew to Xi'an to launch another 'bandit suppression' campaign against the Red Army upriver in Yanan. What happened in Xi'an on 12 December 1936 is still a matter of dispute. But the Young Marshal grabbed the Generalissimo and forced him to talk to the communists' arch-diplomat, Zhou Enlai. The two enemies and the Young Marshal hammered out an agreement that welded all Chinese armies into one command. When the Japanese launched their all-out attack on China a few months later, the arrangement helped save the land. The Xi'an Incident, as it is known in the history books, was one of the most significant events to take place in the city in the 5000 years it has been inhabited. But there are few monuments to it today. Drum towers, pagodas, temples, shrines and mosques hark back to earlier times.

The past that left so rich a cultural foundation is a basis on which China today is building a brand new industry. Only in the past decade has the country seriously engaged in attracting tourists. For many centuries, China was closed to the world, seeking only to live and prosper on its own terms, unsullied by outside contact. The greatest symbol of this, of course, is the Great Wall, designed to withstand barbarian intrusions. But other, more peaceful, visitors were also spurned. When European emissaries arrived respectfully at the Manchu court in the eighteenth century, the emperor received them with good-humoured jocularity, examined them as he might scrutinise some exotic but harmless animals, told them China needed nothing from the outside world and sent them on their way. The rude Scottish traders who disobeyed imperial edicts to run narcotics into China were also rebuffed; but the British reply was to launch warships up the Pearl River, win the Opium War and seize Hongkong. Only in 1978, determined to press

YASUHIRO HAYASHI

*F*ading photographs of Mao's early comrades adorn the wall of a cave home in Shaanxi, not far from the communist headquarters at Yanan.

*L*acy lingerie hangs in a shop window in Pingyao. The consumer revolution sweeping the rest of China is reaching into even the most remote areas.

Right

*M*ost of the goods turned out by the impressive industrial advances of recent years are snapped up by China's enormous domestic market, a billion people with money to spend. In a department store in Taiyuan, capital of Shanxi, strollers eye the goods. For the first time in memory, many have money to spend on luxuries; and for the first time shops have consumer goods to sell.

Overleaf

*S*culpted by the wind into rounded dunes, the sands of the Tengger Desert look deceptively mild. But it is an unforgiving terrain offering little to humanity but its lonely beauty.

TSUGUSATO OMURA

ahead with the Four Modernisations and forge China into a strong industrialised society, did the Chinese government encourage full-scale tourism.

The reasons for this were more complex than at first they appear. On the surface, it is a matter of simple economics; tourism was the cheapest and most efficient way in which to swiftly get a large amount of hard foreign currency needed to buy modern scientific and technological equipment. But there were other reasons. More tourists meant that the Chinese people, for so long cut off from any foreign or modern influences, would be more prepared to face the new era foreseen by the national leaders. And tourism boosts quickly the vital infrastructure needed for any modern economy; it helped to provide more roads, new hotels and better telecommunications.

A great deal of this gamble on tourism as a source of ideas and finance was focused on illuminating China's magnificent past, much of it concentrated along the valley of the Huanghe. Xi'an became the hub of a huge tourist industry that catered for those with a fascination for the ancient dynasties. Qinshihuang may have unified China twenty-two centuries ago, but in the modern era his ghost has also played an important part in helping to finance the rebuilding of the nation because of the torrent of tourist dollars flowing in from those travelling up the Yellow River to examine his tomb. The same was true of other historic sites along the course of the river. As the great tourist influx continued, some of the more adventurous visitors left the comfort of their newly built luxury hotels in Xi'an and ventured upriver to the last resting places of less famous rulers. There were plenty to choose from, especially to the north of Xi'an in the little-known land of Ordos, enclosed by the Great Bend of the Huanghe.

Across the Ordos stand half-buried memorials to a past perceived but dimly through centuries of invasion and warfare. Steep pyramids, their glittering enamel coverings collapsed or pilfered centuries ago, mark the last resting places of long-forgotten kings of races swept away by the flood of history. Shards of pottery in the desert sands carry unreadable messages in ideograms or scripts nobody for a score of generations has been able to read. The traveller in this mystic land where legend still lives recalls the lines of Percy Bysshe Shelley who wrote:

My name is Ozymandias, King of Kings
Look on my works, ye mighty, and despair!
Nothing besides remains. Round the decay
Of that colossal wreck, boundless and bare
The low and level sands stretch far away.

Shelley might have been writing of the Ordos today where the sands stretch far away from mysteries that hint of proud tribes, triumphant nations, past glories, all of them now unremembered, effaced by time and wind, buried by loess and sand, dimly recalled in legend and footnotes of history.

TSUGUSATO OMURA

*W*ith a long crook instead of a short bow, this modern Mongol is a shepherd, not a fighter. But even today, Mongols of the steppes pride themselves on their horsemanship. Tiny, rugged Mongolian ponies like this, protected from winter's howling gales by shaggy coats, carried the armies of Genghis Khan to the ends of the earth.

Left

*F*rom his tomb on the Ordos plains, Genghis Khan stares ferociously down the centuries. Now housed in a new blue and yellow mausoleum, the tomb of the conqueror was constructed after his earlier resting place was badly damaged by Red Guards during the Cultural Revolution. Born into a minor nomad tribe, Temujin welded together the Mongol horsemen into a mobile nation of cavalrymen whose banners triumphantly waved over the greatest land empire the world has ever seen.

The Huns ruled here. Remains of their fortresses stand still, poking through the shifting earth. In those days, fifteen centuries ago and more, the land was fertile and was a staging ground for seven centuries of dispute as Hun and Han battled for the Ordos and the rich lands along the river. Then rose the Western Xia, a kingdom of some intellectual merit where poets developed their own script and architects raised brick palaces and temples clad with coloured tiles. Like Ozymandias, their works were mighty once but known no more; as with many other nations and civilisations, the Xia and all their works were swept away by the horrific ferocity of the Great Khan, Genghis. Temujin, as he was known once and is honoured still by his own race, glares with fearsome passivity in the form of a statue at his mausoleum in Ijinhoro. Wine and food are offered to him still in sacrifices. His works were few, he was a conqueror and a destroyer, not a builder. But like Ozymandias, Genghis Khan still challenges the mighty to despair.

The middle course of the river from Inner Mongolia down to Henan is one of the powerhouses of the nation. The Yellow River may not produce much electricity. But Shanxi coal makes up for the river's weakness. Under its thick cloak of loess, geologists estimate about 45 per cent of the province's 156 266 square kilometres is coal. Reserves are estimated at 200 billion tonnes, a third of the nation's total. And good coal. Coal that burns so hot and bright that it is famed not just in China but abroad. Local economic planners like to boast that they have more than a third of China's prime coal supplies. They are using 180 million tonnes of this precious resource annually to fuel industries that use other Shanxi resources like gypsum,

Coal has been hacked from the rich lodes of Shanxi for many centuries. The province boasts a third of the nation's reserves of top-grade coal. Most of the mining is mechanised but in this open pit, the fuel is cut from the face and carried to the surface in the old back-breaking manner.

YASUHIRO HAYASHI

copper, bauxite and asbestos. With steel, chemical and machinery plants and a provincial network of railways, Shanxi's 26 million people are among the most industrialised of all China. But agriculture has an immense presence in the province and, irrigated by the waters of the Huanghe, Shanxi has for centuries been famed for its millet, maize, beans, walnuts and other crops.

Although today Shanxi is known as the coal bin of China, there is evidence that it was in this province that much early agricultural progress was made. Overshadowed by the gigantic cultural monolith of Xi'an and its spectacular historical heritage, Shanxi can with some justification lay claim to its own unique place in history. Curators at the provincial museum in Taiyuan point out that of all the relics in China before the Tang and Song dynasties, no fewer than 70 per cent have been located in Shanxi. Much remains. The province is particularly rich in painted sculptures; some of the most splendid collections in the country are to be found in places like the Jinchi Guanyin Temple outside Taiyuan. Studded with little-known shrines, temples and grottos, Shanxi is a cultural treasury of the past. Surprisingly, much remains intact.

The province has been for more than 2000 years a favoured marching route for barbarians seeking entry into the Chinese heartland. Huns, Jurchens, Tobas, Mongols . . . all manners of invaders sacked and plundered through Shanxi. It is not surprising that Taiyuan holds twenty-seven temples built to the God of War. The god has been active indeed on the upper reaches of the Feng River where Taiyuan's modern factories now stand. Nearby, no trace remains of the former capital of Jinyang, site of countless seiges. The last was in 969 when, after seven decades

HIROYUKI USAMI

Staring from a Pingyao shop is an old English clock. How did it get there, on sale in a town in Shanxi off the well-beaten tourist track? The shopkeeper didn't know; it had been on his shelves for many years.

TSUGUSATO OMURA

*T*he iron plant at Baotou is one of China's largest. Coal has been mined in the region for centuries and Baotou has developed into Inner Mongolia's second largest city on the riches it has brought.

SEIGO OTSUKA

Above and right

On the headwaters of the Wei River, Buddhist carvers began 1500 centuries ago to axe niches in the sheer precipice of Corn Rock Mountain. Baroque holes and grottos house countless Buddhas. Because the loess earth is so soft, harder rock was carved elsewhere and carried to the artificial caves.

Previous pages

Where Genghis Khan once rode, the steelworks of Baotou now dominate views of the Huanghe in Inner Mongolia. Iron and coal from nearby deposits makes rearing chimneys signposts to new prosperity as furnaces spew out a significant percentage of China's steel production. The city of 800 000 is an industrial oddity amid the open grasslands of the high steppes. On the fringes of the suburbs, Mongol herdsmen still tend their flocks.
TSUGUSATO OMURA

of ceaseless war and invasion and usurpation, the people of Jinyang refused to recognise the new dynasty of Song. Enraged, Emperor Tai Zu blocked the river, threw up dams and canals that diverted the water to drown Jinyang. The siege lasted seven years before the imperial armies marched off to do battle with less stubborn enemies. But they came back, five armies strong, and in 979 the Song armies put the city to the torch, the inhabitants to the sword. Then they once more diverted the waters to wash away the ruins and the ashes. Today, no trace remains.

But such precious buildings as the Wooden Pagoda in Yingxian county remained miraculously intact, as did the grottos at Yungang where 51 000 statues from a few centimetres to 17 metres stare out of the honeycombed cliffs. From along the Feng River came three saintly early emperors of legendary antiquity: Yao, who invented the calendar in about 2356 BC and appointed Commissioner Yu to regulate watercourses in 2286 BC; Shun who instituted examinations for public officials in 2224 BC; and Yu the Great, credited with first taming the Huanghe in about 2205 AD. Memorials to the three are still standing today.

Proof of religion and belief is everywhere to be found along the middle reaches of the Huanghe. It was down the river that Buddhism came to China, along the Silk Road that traders brought Nestorian Christianity from Syria and Islam from Arabia and Judaism from Baghdad. Islam flourished mightily until the great religious wars of the 1860s when a civil uprising notable for its ferocity on both sides left only 60 000 Islamic survivors of Shaanxi's estimated 800 000 faithful. These days, the call to prayer can be heard once again. Taoism was perfected here, born of the mystic notions of man living in harmony with nature. Shrines, temples, mosques, memorials and museums all stand in evidence of the influence of philosophy and thought. Emperors of the Yin (2000 BC) consulted the gods frequently. They wrote messages on tortoise shells, cast them into hot fires and interpreted the answers by the way in which the heat cracked the lines of written characters. About a fifth of the ideograms have been deciphered by modern scholars who hope, one day, to be able to say what messages their ancient gods had for the kings of Yin.

The flood of tourist dollars attracted by the past is being used to finance an industrial future, to build a society that ancient soothsayers could never have visualised from messages on charred tortoise shells. The age of hi-tech flowers within sight of ancient tombs. Shaanxi scientists and engineers build modern aircraft, make telecommunication satellite receivers and invent computers, while technicians run heavy industrial plants that make diesel engines, machine tools and medical equipment. The province remains famous for its arts and craft, however, many of which were first invented here. Ceramics, cloisonné, bronze and woven willow-ware are among the noted handicrafts of modern Shaanxi, many of whose 30 million people maintain a deep interest in the cultures of the past so evident in

TSUGUSATO OMURA

A nation on wheels, China is a land of 200 million bicycles. In Baotou, the largest city in Mongolia, thousands pedal down a broad avenue to begin their daily work.

Right

*V*illage crafts made by young girls decorate homes near the headwaters of the Wei River. Local tradition calls for mothers to pass on skills such as paper cutting to their daughters, who then proudly display their handiwork in the windows of their homes.

the southern half of the province. The 195 000 square kilometres of Shaanxi range from lush forested land in the south to deeply eroded, arid loess deserts in the north, beyond the farthest vestiges of the Great Wall.

As the river comes out of Mongolia and hacks through the loess lands, creating the border between Shaanxi and Shanxi, its character changes once again. As each new stream adds a generous donation of mud and silt, the colour gets richer, more golden in the sun, sullen brown where it runs in the shadows of the rearing earthen banks 100 metres high, standing like castled ramparts 200 metres apart. Between these natural dykes, the waters run sometimes placidly, often in turbulent waves, always with unpredictable moods. Bridges are few, ferries frail. On the higher hills above the river, unseen from the banks, run the savaged lands which for centuries have provided raw material for nature's artistry. The few but fierce summer downpours have carved the hills into fantastic shapes. Winds whistling down from the northern steppes have helped shape pillars, frescoed cliff faces and carved etchings on the side of hills. Bizarre, weird earthscapes that look, wrote one traveller a century ago, as though they belong on another planet. Plunging through the gorges, the river emerges into wide plains, flows easily across the flatlands only to cut once more through narrow confines in the hills. At Hukou Falls, the flood pours in an ochre fury over steps of limestone, crashing 20 metres over a wide front with a roar that peasants claim can be heard 15 kilometres away. Such is the load of silt that, as the spray is hurled into the air, the sunshine gleams through yellow vapour.

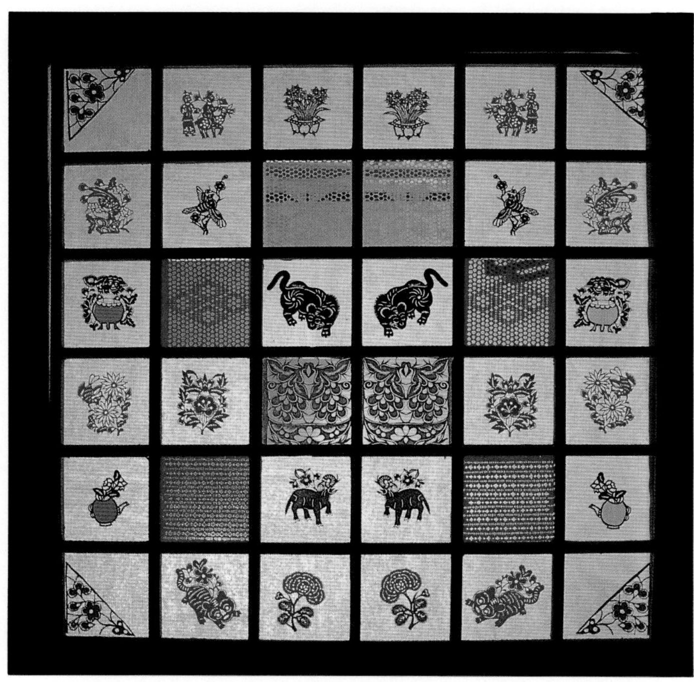

SEIGO OTSUKA

黄土高原

THE LOESS LANDS

HIGH IN THE ravaged gullies of the loess plateau, over an area as large as the United Kingdom, hundreds of thousands of peasant farmers who have never seen the Huanghe are helping to cut down the risk of floods along the lower courses of the river. They are doing so with shovel and seedlings, planting forests of the future that will in years to come prevent further horrendous erosion of the soft loess soil. Scientists estimate that a square kilometre of land in these steep rain-lashed gullies can every year lose up to 35 000 tonnes of soil. Most of this is carried down streams to tributaries then on to the Yellow River. There it is dumped on the riverbed, helping to build up the river level as it grows constantly higher than the surrounding plain. To break this eternal vicious circle, new economic policies have aided conservationists to persuade farmers to become keen agents of reforestation on the tired hills of the Shaanxi-Shanxi uplands.

In a modest government ministry building in Zhengzhou, capital of the ancient province of Henan where sixteen dynasties and kingdoms have had their capitals, engineers today ponder a question as old as China itself. How best, ask the men and women at the headquarters of the Yellow River Conservancy Commission, can the Huanghe be tamed? It is a question to which many people have answers. But putting those answers into operation is a problem that faced ancient hydrologists and one that still confronts their successors today. It is the gigantic scale of the problem rather than its complexity that is the major hurdle. Few people know the Huanghe and its infinite moods better than the 28 000-strong staff of the Commission. From the headwaters in Qinghai, where the River Source Research

In what may be the greatest afforestation program in history, people are pressing back the desert. Helped by waters from Yellow River irrigation schemes, these hardy tussocks will hold sand together. Over the years, trees may take hold here.

Like a trick performed by a masterly magician, the Huanghe suddenly appears out of a cleft in the mountains of Qinghai. It has just flowed angrily through the narrowest passage in its entire journey, the Wild Fox Canyon, so called because local tribesmen say the ravine is so narrow that a wild fox has been seen to leap its ten-metre gap.

Unit still seeks to locate branches of the headwaters, down to the Gulf of Bohai where new land is being formed of silt, Commission staff are constantly monitoring the health of the river.

The problem of flooding and its control begins basically where the river enters its second stage of life in the Inner Mongolian Autonomous Region. Here, it carries the beginning of the immense load of silt that will, many kilometres downstream, cause concern to the river managers and constant worry to millions who live near its banks. The situation rapidly gets worse when the Huanghe courses wildly down between Shaanxi and Shanxi provinces. This is the cancerous heartland where savage erosion shifts enormous amounts of soil into the waterway. Studies by Gong Shiyang and Mou Jinze, experts from the Yellow River Commission, have been acclaimed by international hydrologists as definitive examinations on how to combat severe erosion. But although such investigations have shown what needs to be done to control the river and the erosion that is adding to its problems, the huge scope of remedial work is so extensive that engineers are quick to admit that they are far from success. They have made huge strides in recent years with spectacular results. But as Gong Shiyang, Director of the Chinese Society of Hydraulic Engineers has written, you can't change 4000 years of neglect with a mere forty years of toil. There is a long way to go for workers of the Yellow River Commission.

For many centuries the main concern of people living along the river was in looking after themselves. By and large through history, what happened a few kilometres upstream was unknown. Even if anyone had realised that neglect was causing trouble further up the river, there was nothing anyone could have done about it. By the same token, what took place downstream where it did not affect you was none of your concern.

That attitude has long changed. The Yellow River Commission in Zhengzhou, the Ministry of Water Resources and Electrification in Beijing and bureaux and departments in every provincial capital and city along the river are now welded into an overall national effort to bring the Huanghe to heel. The sheer statistics of the problem are immense, yet so are the resources being used to solve them.

Flooding is not the only catastrophe against which engineers plan. Drought can be almost as troublesome, if not as calamitous. Every year, an average 56 billion cubic metres of water flows down the Huanghe. Most of this comes from the upper reaches; almost 60 per cent of the volume of the river comes from above Lanzhou, a mere 30 per cent of the drainage area. As the river rolls north through Gansu on the start of the Great Bend, its character changes; the further it gets downstream, it seems to shrink. This is no illusion. Water is being drawn off from the Huanghe at an incredible rate. As the river bisects the thirsty farmlands, electric pumps labour, ancient waterwheels turn, sluice gates leading to irrigation canals are raised, occasional windmills whirl; all pull water from the river. Before it

SEIGO OTSUKA

*F*rom these scarred and ravaged hills of Shanxi comes much of the loess topsoil washed yearly into the Huanghe. From these cancerous hills comes the silt that ultimately causes disaster far downstream on the plains. Over centuries, layers of silt have laid down a high, ever-growing base atop which runs the Huanghe. When it bursts its banks, it sweeps wide over the lowland plains.

HIROYUKI USAMI

Like some ornate lacing on the loess hillside, this pavilion of the Five Spring Mountain Park gives unsurpassed views down the valley.

reaches the sea, an astounding 27 billion cubic metres, half the total volume of water in the Huanghe, is taken out. About 11 billion cubic metres is drawn off in the upper reaches before the Yellow River leaves Mongolia's dry grasslands. In the middle stretch down to Zhengzhou a further 6 billion cubic metres are pumped out; and as the Huanghe meanders between its sturdy dykes over the North China Plain another 10 billion cubic metres flow out through sluice gates down from the elevated riverbed to the fertile flatlands below.

The most common means of takeoff from the main stream of the Huanghe is simplicity itself. Because the river has over centuries been continuously building up its bed at a rate of about 10 centimetres a year along the lower stretches, the river as it runs between its strong dykes can be up to 10 metres above the level of surrounding plains. This is the situation near Kaifeng, in northeastern Henan, where the bed of the river is well above the rooftop level of the ancient city. So when irrigation water is needed critically in the dry months of the early growing season in May, June and July, before the plains get their summer rains, staff manning the sluice gates just have to push a button. Powerful electric motors turn huge screws which raise the steel sluice gates set strongly into the sides of the dykes. The water flows out smoothly into canals which run through the fields, gravity taking off the spillage into a thousand smaller watercourses to ditches that lead the trickles to tens of thousands of fields.

In this way, 80 million *mou* of land (about 5.5 million hectares) receive inexpensive and reliable irrigation. In much the same manner have the fields been watered for 4000 years during which, despite flood, despite drought, despite disasters of all kinds, the Huanghe has supported massive populations. A third of all arable land in the river drainage system is under some form of irrigation.

This drain on the river leads to the ironic situation that the Yellow River is becoming increasingly short of water. Statistics show that in every June between 1972 and 1981, there were periods when the Huanghe was dry. These totalled 118 days in the nine years and at times the 500-kilometre stretch of riverbed between Li Jing and Luo Kou was barely damp between long pools of quiet water and silted banks. For river planners, this is a situation almost as unpalatable as uncontrollable flooding, and the huge series of dams and reservoirs built upstream may help to keep the water level more even at every season along the length of the river.

But even more drastic measures were foreseen in the mid-1980s when national planners considered the contradictory problem of China's Sorrow, the river that had drowned millions, being regularly short of water. One dramatic scheme was a plan to divert part of the huge flow of the Yangtze River up new channels parallel to the Grand Canal to flow into the lower reaches of the Huanghe and guarantee water to the peasants of Shandong – not as bizarre as may be first thought, because in a previous reincarnation the Huanghe flowed down this way

SEIGO OTSUKA

As it flows near the city of Xining, the Huanghe seems a placid waterway, belying the periodic and overwhelming destruction it can cause to those who live and work along its banks.

Overleaf

Loyally following their leader, sheep nimbly tread in the track of their shepherd to cross the frozen tributary near Jiaxian in Shaanxi province.

SEIGO OTSUKA

*A*gainst a backdrop of loess earth, a Shanxi peasant family and its donkey cart present an ageless tableau of China.

and found its way to the sea through the Huai and Yangtze Rivers. Such a plan, at a cost of RMB40 billion, was seen by planners as a viable solution to the problem of the empty watercourse.

If it comes to pass, the comparatively cleaner waters of the Yangtze might help solve the clogging influence of sediment that bedevils the lower reaches of the Huanghe. When staff at some of the 474 hydrometric measuring stations on the Huanghe take specimens of water to examine, they generally scoop up a cubic metre of the murky solution. When the silt settles, they find on average that every cubic metre of water from the river contains an astonishing 37.6 kilograms of soil. Other major rivers are lazy indeed compared to the formidable loads carried by the Yellow River. The Ganges holds only a tenth as much, 3.9 kilograms per cubic metre, the muddy Nile a mere 1.4, the Amazon a miniscule 0.07, the Mississippi 0.6, the Indus 4.3. The only river that comes even close to the Huanghe is the Colorado with 27.5 kilograms of sediment in every cubic metre of water. But the Colorado does not run through a plain 800 kilometres wide populated by scores of millions of people.

The first, primary aim of the Central Government, the Yellow River Commission and the provincial authorities is to halt, or, anyway, slow down, the frightening erosion eating away at the barren hills of Shaanxi-Shanxi. The Yellow River drains 752 000 square kilometres, and of this, 430 000 has been eroded, 236 000 seriously. The reasons are simple: over the centuries forests have been cut down, vegetation destroyed by overgrazing, and hillsides overworked by the plough and not terraced to slow down the runoff of summer rains. All contributed to erosion. Together, these causes have made the land weak, unable to withstand the pounding of rain storms. The trouble-prone Shaanxi hills get an annual average of 500 millimetres of rain, but most of this can come in a few blinding storms. Once a fissure has opened in the wounded land, a couple of storms swiftly eat into the soft loess and cut deeply. Conservationists say that up to 10 000 tonnes of loess soil can be washed away from each square kilometre of land every year, and in gullies it can reach a desperate rate of 35 000 tonnes.

Teams of soil control workers have for decades tramped these bare hills to see what can be done. Work gangs of thousands of men and women marched in brigades over the same hills in the 1950s and 1960s, forming terraces to prevent erosion, planting trees and shrubs. But while real progress was made between 1949 and 1979, it has only been in the last few years that great strides have taken place. The reason is obvious: money. Ordering reorganisation of peasant farmers in 1978, China's Supreme Leader Deng Xiaoping threw out the old communal work system and put the people to work for themselves under contract arrangements. This meant, broadly speaking, that the harder people worked, the more they produced, and the more money they made. The effects of these simple but revolu-

HIROYUKI USAMI

Where irrigation takes water to the terraces, the stark eroded hills of Gansu flash with brilliant greenery. In an enormous afforestation program, huge areas of these scarred highlands that cover Gansu, Shanxi, Shaanxi and parts of Ningxia and Mongolia have been planted with trees. But it will take years before the new vegetation takes proper hold, spreading roots that will bind together the fragile loess soil and leaves that will provide some shelter from the summer downpours that cause so much erosion in the highlands.

*I*n the hot sun of autumn, farmers lay crops over country roads, hoping that passing traffic will do some of their work. Trucks and carts help break the grain from the chaff, making easier the back-breaking work of winnowing the crop.

Right

A human scarecrow sits under a makeshift shelter from the summer sun, ready to beat gongs, shout and throw stones to chase away birds which may be attracted to the watermelons growing in the irrigated fields near Xi'an. The Wei River waters have brought verdant life to these well-tilled fields since before the dawn of the first dynasty.

tionary procedures in agriculture were immediate; within five years, without spending a *fen* of government money, China's agricultural production doubled in value, merely because people worked harder and more efficiently for themselves than for the communes. The new regulations were to have an equally dramatic effect on flood control and erosion prevention measures on the Yellow River.

From the start of the 1980s, production brigades in areas troubled by persistent serious erosion have been assigning blocks of land on long contract to peasant households. The leases are for up to twenty years and generally cover between 3 and 6 hectares of land, sprawling areas by the standards of Chinese flatland agriculture. But these are not the rich fertile plains where every square metre of arable land is planted and petted; in these hills, long denuded of trees, the heavy cloudbursts of summer have carved deep and treacherous patterns, and it is from the eroded uplands of Gansu, Ningxia, Shaanxi and Shanxi that the bulk of the loess has been stripped which causes so much trouble when it is dumped as silt in the riverbed on the plains. That problem of silting is what is being tackled today by granting farmers long leases which call for them to plant certain numbers of specific kinds of trees.

Willows and pines and fruit trees, shrubs that bear fodder for their livestock, all the plants have certain features in common. They are all hardy species of vegetation which can withstand long drought. More importantly, they all have deep, seeking roots which penetrate far into the loess soil and hold the earth together. All have heavy foliage that breaks the force of the pounding rains which have scoured the earth. The key to the plan is profit. In twenty years, the trees will have grown and some can be felled for lumber, producing a substantial cash crop for the rural families. For them, it is money in the bank. For the Chinese economy, the effects will also be significant because after centuries of neglect an area of 65 000 square kilometres (about as big as Ireland or West Virginia) is becoming productive.

The most severely eroded area, 7000 square kilometres of nightmare hills and gullies, has been terraced at enormous effort and turned into a national park. With young trees still growing, the land remains too delicate to permit the open entry of people and the area will remain restricted for years to come until nature clothes it in an abundant cover of protective vegetation. Yellow River conservancy staff claim proudly that this is the first move in breaking the eternal vicious cycle of rain, erosion, silting, dumping, river-raising, flood and disaster, a string of connected events that has led to tragedy for as long as humans have dwelt on the river's banks.

By helping to eliminate the bane of erosion, hydrologists hope to solve further problems downstream. The main one is to halt soil slipping from the gullies of the loess plateau into the streams, and hence into the tributaries and the Huanghe. The best hope of doing this is in the steeply cut valleys where erosion begins, and – as with the successful tree-planting exercise – this is being tackled with a combina-

The old walled city of Pingyao in Shanxi is a living museum, one of the last towns in China still contained within its stout walls. Until recent times, walls were necessary in this lawless land where bandits roamed and rival warlord armies fought to control whole provinces. In these more tranquil times, most walls have been demolished. Where they remain, the stout fortifications are a memory of more dangerous times.

tion of education and economic rewards. In a thousand upland valleys, peasants are being encouraged to throw small dams and reservoirs across streams. These stay the flood of fierce summer runoffs down through gullies, and the water held in series of dams contains high percentages of silt. Gradually, in the course of two or three years, the reservoirs behind the dams fill with silt and compact into new flat fields. Once planted with crops, these provide natural protection against the wild torrential runoffs, slowing the once-harmful mad flood of water into a less-damaging flow.

Scientists claim that almost every gram of silt carried out of the gullies ends up on the bed of the Yellow River. By helping some farmers to terrace hillsides and build catchment dams, conservancy staff have given an example which other farmers, quick to see the obvious financial advantage of nature creating fertile arable flat land for them, have been swift to follow. In recent years, spurred on by the money they can make by selling the produce of private fields, the peasants have erected countless new dams which taken together have significantly aided in reducing erosion and staunching the seep of silt downstream. Conservationists estimate that 28 500 square kilometres of land in Gansu, Shaanxi and Shanxi (an area about the size of Belgium or Maryland) has been terraced in recent years. More than a quarter million hectares of new flat land have been created behind dams built by peasants in steep gullies.

Combined, these moves have had dramatic results downstream. By studying layers of silt, historical records and the banks of dykes and by interviewing venerable local residents, scientists and engineers compute that since 1919 an average of 1.6 billion tonnes of silt have every year been carried down the Huanghe. Of this, 1.2 billion tonnes have been flushed out to sea, where much of it sinks gently into the Gulf of Bohai to form new areas of China around the estuary at the rate of 23.5 square kilometres a year.

But a troublesome 400 million tonnes a year of silt have been deposited yearly on the bed of the river. And it is here that the major cause of trouble begins. Judging by the average figures since 1919, engineers in the mid-1980s could claim some success. In 1986, a mere 200 million tonnes of silt were laid on the bed of the river. To some, this could be regarded as proof of spectacular success of anti-erosion measures in the middle reaches. But at the computer centre at Zhengzhou, engineers cautiously point out to visitors that this low level came in a year of less-than-average rainfall. In 1977, they remind each other, when fierce summer downpours lashed the Shaanxi-Shanxi hills, the river dropped a worrying 900 million tonne load. And they look back to the big flood of 1933 when raging waters left behind an incredible 3.7 billion tonnes of silt in Henan and Shandong. They agree they are pleased so far with the progress made in soil control and erosion prevention techniques, but they stress that this is merely the start and that a lot of muddy water will come down the Yellow River before erosion is under control.

SEIGO OTSUKA

*L*ost in the immensity of the river, a ferry with red flags snapping in the wind ploughs over the Huanghe from Shaanxi to Shanxi. Despite the age of many of the craft and their apparent frailty, accidents are rare, thanks in part to the skill of the riverboat men who spend their lives on the turbulent, changeable waters.

Carrying bicycles, produce and people, local farmers trek across a narrow ford on the Wei stream in Gansu province.

Right

In treeless Shaanxi, building materials are scarce and costly. Long ago villagers in Chianlin came to a logical conclusion and burrowed beneath their fields to dig their homes. Similar solutions to the same problem have been developed independently throughout the flat plains loess where there are no handy hills into which to dig cave dwellings. To make sunken villages like Yaotong, farmers dig a deep, square hole. They then cut into the sides of the excavation to build their homes. The original excavation becomes a comfortable courtyard.

The problem, and the prosperity of much of North China, comes from the light yellow soil of which most of the region is built. For millions of years before the first life appeared on earth, successive changes in the climate were preparing the geological foundations of the Yellow River valley. In ice ages so long and severe that scientists still find it difficult to comprehend their scope, sheets of glaciers as large as continents ground their way over the surface of the globe. As their grim passages came and went, they reduced much of the lava and granite to boulders, then rubble, then dust. Over the ages, successive changes in climate – heat and cold, wet and dry – further reduced the size of these particles. Then the constant prevailing winds picked up these fine motes, whirled them high in the air and carried them eastwards, across Siberia, over Central Asia. As the winds weakened, the dust dropped to settle gently over what is now the catchment area of the Yellow River. The provinces of Qinghai, Gansu, Shaanxi, Shanxi, Henan and much of Shandong, the northern reaches of Jiangsu and Anhui, the autonomous regions of Ningxia and large areas of Mongolia all bear deep layers of this windborne soil.

It is a process that lasted millions of years. It continues today. The extremes of heat and cold in the high plains of Central Asia, up to 50 degrees Celsius in summer, down to −30 degrees in winter, cause constant decomposition of rock. More dust is created ceaselessly. Just as ceaselessly, the winds scoop it up and send it eastwards. In historical times it has buried known landmarks, and in the dry winters today it is the loess from the steppes of Central Asia causing the gritty dust storms that plague Beijing and other northern cities. The dust, as it comes down, is a dull greyish-ochre hue. When it is wet, the colour darkens. Suspended in water, it gives the liquid a murky yellow tinge. When the water is in a river, the colour seems to lighten, to become brighter, a shade between light brown and, when the sun is in the right direction, a golden glow. It is the loess that gives the Yellow River its colour and its name.

Travelling today through the loess uplands and the North China Plain – both regions that owe their existence to the fine dust – the observer sometimes finds it difficult to tell where the architecture of nature ends and the handiwork of mankind starts. Adobe brick walls plastered with mud blend into bland, stoneless cliffs of the compressed soil. What part was designed by humans, what part constructed by nature? The difference is often slight. The curious can break off a piece of loess from any riverbank or roadside cutting and examine for themselves the earth on which North China arose. If wet, the soil dissolves into mud. If dry, a child can crumble it easily back into the dust from which it was formed. It is featureless earth except where erosion has carved the landscape into bizarre and tortured shapes.

The earliest agriculturalists of prehistoric China found it easy to work the fine yellow soil. They knew early how much to prize its fertility. It is no coincidence

HIROYUKI USAMI

*F*ilms, radio, television and nationwide lessons in Putonghua, the national tongue, are helping to spread one standard form of Chinese speech throughout the country. Local dialects are still commonly used at home, but because of standardised schooling, people from one end of the Huanghe valley to the other can now understand each other – for the first time in history.

Previous pages

*S*cratching a living from eroded slopes, farmers are careful to maintain the terraces built over the centuries. Acting as temporary dams to stop the corrosive flow of summer downpours, the stepped earth of the hillsides prevents rains from carrying silt into the streams and rivers that flow into the Huanghe. Where rain can attack raw earth on such steep slopes, it carries away up to 35 000 tonnes of soil every year from a single square kilometre.
YASUHIRO HAYASHI

that the part of the Great Wall across dry northern Shanxi and Shaanxi is built almost along the line where tillable loess deposits peter out into the harsh steppes of Central Asia. This side of the Wall erected by the Ming was the Chinese world; stable, arable, serene. Outside, beyond the fertile loess soil, was the domain of the barbarians; lawless, nomadic, dangerous. The Yellow River suckled the infant Chinese nation, and it was weaned on the rich loess dropped by the winds of ages.

The study of loess was not a subject to which ancient Chinese scholars seemingly paid a great deal of attention. The land was there; they pondered what to do with it rather than wondering from whence it came. But a century ago, westerners pushing into the loess provinces paid a great deal of attention indeed to the phenomenon of the land created by wind. Most of those quizzical scientists were Germans or Russians, their doyen a doughty and enquiring Prussian, Dr E.F. von Richthofen. He originated the theory of ice and wind being the basic forces that created and transported the dusty earth of northern China. His teachings were followed up in later decades by enthusiastic biologists, historians, geologists and agriculturalists. For scientists in every discipline the loess lands held huge fascination, as they do today for the curious tourist.

Von Richthofen claimed that some of the loess deposits were as thick as 1000 metres and were laid down over millions of years. Estimates by later scientists fortunate enough to have modern geological equipment showed that the layers were not so deep. The wind-laid dust deposits have been shown to be 100 metres thick over huge swathes of northern China. Depths of 600 metres have been found before drillers reached the carboniferous and limestone bedrock layers on which the loess rests.

What von Richthofen did not realise was that this impenetrable blanket was laid down over existing invisible landscapes of mountains, plains and valleys. The densest layer of this geological freak is in the central region of the Huanghe, the most extensive area of its type on earth. The loess plateau, as it is generally known, forms a continuous ochre blanket more than 1000 kilometres from west to east and up to 400 kilometres north to south. Roughly speaking, the Yellow River runs across the middle of this rich blanket of soil. And almost in the middle, near where the Wei River runs into the superior flow of the Huanghe, is the area where the forerunners of the Chinese people dug into the good earth to plant their crops and sink their racial roots.

The cliffside layers of loess that can be seen in the steep river gorges of Shaanxi and Shanxi provide fascinating reading for biological detectives. The dirt holds many chapters of the natural past, and fossil remains of such creatures show that in warmer times rhinoceros, elephants, lions and hippopotamuses were happily at home in northern China. In some areas, fossil remains are so rich that construction workers cutting roads may reveal white layers of bone amid the deep

HIROYUKI USAMI

Crowds bustle in the Pingyao street market. The protective walls around the town are built on the ruins of fortifications finished thirty centuries ago. Later, more imposing walls, still clad in brick, stand today, eleven metres high and five metres thick.

*B*usy in a private factory, this woman spins wood fibre into a material that will be used to make boots.

banks of yellow soil. Particularly common fossils are the eggs of ostriches, which were once common on the plains. In 1923, archaeologist J.G. Anderson writing in the *Far Eastern Review* counted eighteen sites yielding forty-four authenticated eggs of ostriches. They must have been big birds; one egg measured 193 millimetres. Ostriches had long gone by the time the first humans appeared on the banks of the Huanghe. But from time to time, floods or earthquakes or excavations or well diggings would unveil one of the big eggs. To the superstitious villagers who found such remnants of the unknown past, it was logical what they were; legend told them the river was a dragon and these were obviously dragon eggs.

It is the cultivators of China who owe the biggest debt to the loess lands. Here is fine, fertile soil, earth that takes naturally to the plough, land free of rocks and boulders which could hurt oxen and blunt iron shares. The soil is kind to farmers. Rich in lime, potash, phosphorus and other minerals, the loess holds water well in the dry seasons. Comes the spring, and the thaw sends winter's ice and snow seeping into the soil just in time to benefit most the new-planted crops. The heavy summer rains of the loess plateau do not leach the soil of vital minerals; indeed, horticulturists claim the water washes minerals to the top, making the soil virtually self-enriching. Organic manure helps keep the soil productive.

*I*n angry years, the Huanghe rises to cover completely the long sandbank of Niangniangtan which lies, more than a kilometre long, between Shanxi and Shaanxi near the city of Hequ. But farmers like this couple refuse to move. The lush crops of maize and other produce they raise on the rich silt deposits convince them that bumper harvests are worth the risks of periodic flood.

The farmers along the Huanghe often get more than one opportunity to use the good earth. Just as constant winds bring eternal replenishment of soil windborne from Central Asia so do the river waters carry the soil particles downstream, leaving rich deposits of silt downriver in dry seasons. Within the high levees that guard the lower 1400 kilometres of the Yellow River, farmers are quick to plant crops when the waters are at a low level, hoping to be able to pick a bumper harvest of swift-growing vegetables before the rising waters claim the crops. And at the mouth of the river, the muddy waters reach the sea and drop their heavy burden of silt, creating 23.5 square kilometres of new land every year. This process has been going on since 1853 when the river last changed course and flowed out of the present channel. In a few years, as the mouth of the river extends a couple of kilometres further into the brackish waters of the Gulf of Bohai, the land being created today will itself be turned into productive farmland. The new land originated more than half a continent away in Soviet Central Asia, was blown thousands of kilometres to be dropped on the loess plateau, then transported by courtesy of the silt-laden Yellow River the final 2400 kilometres from the eroded gullies of Shaanxi to create this newest small corner of China.

TSUGUSATO OMURA

Every available worker turns out to bring in the golden harvest of wheat, staple food of northern China, near Zhongning, Ningxia.

The Chinese farmers know well how to take care of this good earth. Over thousands of years they have developed techniques to protect and enrich their fields. Irrigation from the river is in itself an efficient means of fertilising the soil. As the waters are diverted or pumped into the fields, they carry in suspension an enormous load of soil and minerals.

The eminent Professor Chang Gee-yuen estimated the average silt content of the river at 11 per cent. The writer Chang Jung in the early Han dynasty reckoned it to be between 6 and 10 per cent. An American scientist, Professor W. C. Lowdermilk, who studied the question of silt in various stretches of the Yellow River while teaching at Nanjing University in the 1920s, carried out detailed experiments at the time of flooding. He took 1-litre samples of water from the river on three separate occasions just after the peak of floodwaters had passed. Then he filtered the samples, dried the residue at 100°C and weighed it. To his amazement and the astonishment of fellow scientists when his report was published in scholarly journals, he discovered his samples had yielded between 14 and 22 per cent silt by weight. This is something that peasant farmers knew instinctively centuries ago.

Throughout the length of the river and its tributaries, silted waters have been much sought after for irrigation. Long before communes were introduced, peasants would cooperate to build canals to divert floodwaters, then guide the mud-laden water to their fields. Once the water lay still amid the crops, the muddy sediment with its rich load of minerals would soon sink. The canny farmers knew they were not only providing water for the crop that was growing but also enriching the land with fertiliser for crops not yet planted.

YASUHIRO HAYASHI

*C*arved layer upon layer, burrowing deeply into the loess hillsides, rows of homes are dug into the cliffs of Kaoxikou in Shaanxi province.

More than 2000 years ago farmers along the Ching River in central Shanxi, an area noted even then for its efficient irrigation system, were singing this song:

A tan of Ching water contains much silt
It irrigates and it fertilises
It makes your crop grow
It feeds millions in the country's capital

The same sentiment was expressed somewhat more succinctly by the conservationist minister in charge of economics in the Tang dynasty, who urged peasants to dredge the waters of the Po canal to supply their fields with both water and fertiliser. This was a fact that imperial mandarin and foreign academic did not need to impress on Chinese peasant farmers. They had lived through hard times to learn the lesson, because it was a fact of life grimly obvious to every survivor of a famine. When the Huanghe or a silted tributary flooded, water covered the land and destroyed the crops. After the water level retreated, it left a thick layer of silt. There was nothing to eat the following winter, or very little, and a large percentage of the population perished. But ironically, the next autumn would bring forth a bumper crop, a bursting richness of the earth, often more than those who had lived through the hungry year could bring themselves to eat. The farmers of old may not have had degrees in agricultural science, but they had eyes that could see and bellies that rumbled with hunger when the Yellow River misbehaved.

The curse of the loess lands is the cancer of erosion. In Gansu, Shaanxi and Shanxi where the deposits are thickest, rivers and streams have cut the soft earth into weird designs. Nature, the great artist, has carved bizarre shapes from the grainless material. It is, much of it, a land tortured by wind and rain and running water into agonising shape. The landscape looks hacked as though by some deranged monstrous giant amok with an axe. It crumbles, defenceless, before the elements, falls into the streams and chokes the rivers. It is on its progress down the Shaanxi-Shanxi border that the Huanghe picks up more than half its immense load of silt. Behind, it leaves a nightmare landscape of earth that has been scarred irreparably by steep gullies and deep ravines. The erosion eats swiftly into the hills, each rainfall causing more extensive gnawing away of the soil.

The loess provides not only fertile land. In some parts of Shanxi it also puts a roof over the head of peasant families. The best-known example is Yanan on the Yan River where at the end of the Long March Mao Zedong and his surviving revolutionaries made their homes for a decade in cave houses cut from the cliffs. 'Warm in winter, cool in summer,' Mao boasted to the few visitors who made the dangerous journey to Yanan in the years the communists were fighting both the Japanese and the Guomindang army of Jiang Kaishek.

Millions of people still live in caves in the loess lands today for reasons not only of economy but also of comfort. In a land without trees, lumber is expensive.

*R*ape flowers blossom amid the fields surrounding a Yaotong village.

So is other building material, apart from adobe bricks made from the loess itself. Far easier in areas with cliffs cut by erosion to burrow into the hillsides. Such cave dwellings are not temporary shelters but expansive, permanent homes.

At most times, they are safe from flood and other hazard. But compacted as the loess earth can be, cave houses can be inherently dangerous in areas where historical annals record huge earthquakes. It was such a quake that rocked Shanxi viciously in AD 1290, which is still regarded as the greatest natural disaster of all time; contemporary records put the death toll at a staggering 12 million. Some died when their loess roofs collapsed on them, others in flooding caused by land damming the rivers, probably most from starvation in the subsequent famine. Chroniclers of every dynasty stud their yearly records of the loess lands with terse accounts of 'mountain slips' after earthquakes .

Left

Valued for the oil from its pressed seeds, a crop of rape glows as it nears time for harvest in Qinghai.

SEIGO OTSUKA

A welcoming glow from a loess cliff-face signals home and comfort to those who live in these houses in the hillsides of the village of Kaoxikou in Shaanxi.

代代洪水為患

DISASTERS OF THE DYNASTIES

IN 2297 BC, the Huanghe rose in calamitous flood. The results were catastrophic. An official named Kuan was named Minister of Works charged with safeguarding the empire against the ravages of the river on which depended the very existence of the people. Minister Kuan laboured mightily, but eight years after his appointment the river once again rampaged, broke its banks and submerged the land. Two years later the luckless Kuan was banished, and in the imperial decrees of 2286 BC one of the four appointments (others were agriculture, education and fire) was that of Minister Yu who was charged with regulating the watercourses of the realm. Since the very birth of the Chinese state, control of the Huanghe has been paramount in the minds of its rulers. 'Who controls the Yellow River controls China,' stated Yu the Great, the ruler credited with first bringing effective forms of flood control to the Huanghe 4200 years ago. Since then much of the energies and initiatives of rule have been bent to the task of controlling the river, of making the waters obey the will of human beings. For most of this time, these efforts have been in vain. And built with horrific loss of life. In AD 605, ministers of the Sui court impressed 200 000 men to build a canal near Xi'an; such was the frenzy of the imperial overseers that half the men were worked to death.

Flood followed by famine has been a dreary regular occurrence in the history of the river. Only in the past three decades has the mighty torrent been brought under control. Today, officials in Beijing boast with pride, the dragon has been at least partially tamed. Of all the achievements of the People's Republic, possibly none is pointed to with greater satisfaction than the conquest of the Yellow River. It

*F*lowing between the twin lakes of Ngoring and Gyaring, the Yellow River turns to silver. The land here is swampy, windswept and desolate, a harsh environment for the nomadic peoples who continue to roam the plains.

HIROYUKI USAMI

A glimpse of beauty amid the misery of the desolate Songpan swamp.

is a victory that ranks with the communists' campaign to eliminate hunger. It is a matter of intense national pride.

The people have four sorrows.
The first is flood, the second drought.
The third is locusts, the final warlords.

– Ancient peasant saying, origin unknown.

China's Sorrow, the river has been called, with much justification. Ancient records tell time and again of the floods that periodically covered the lands, destroying crops, sentencing millions to a slow death by famine. It happened in 2079 BC in the reign of Emperor Shao Kang of the Xia dynasty, and the same horrific scenario was played out in the great Henan famine of 1943 in which three million starved. China's Sorrow . . . never was a river more aptly named.

But flood was not the only natural peril to threaten the lives of those who lived in the great valley and its vast alluvial plains. Calamity came in many forms. Earthquake was one. In 193 BC the earth buckled and shook as Shanxi was racked by a huge quake. It was as though the legendary dragon of the river had awoken. That same year, as banks tumbled into the river and loess cliffs collapsed, drought withered the land. Despairing scholarly reports of the time recall how thunderclouds stalked the countryside, how the seasons were reversed with fruit and flowers appearing in the harsh northern winter. For four years, drought made the waters of the Huanghe even more vital to human survival, and then, as though heaven was punishing the people, the emperor died plunging the reign into a dynastic war broken only by another gigantic earthquake in 186 BC. The following year, much of Henan was inundated by vast flooding and six years later came such a deluge, accompanied by mountains slipping into the river and compounded by earthquakes, that 179 BC is still reckoned as being the Year of the Great Flood.

There are many other years etched in tragedy in the history of the river as the cycle of centuries swung from drought to flood to famine. In 138 BC, floods caused such devastating famine in Shandong that the imperial authorities were appalled by the extent of cannibalism. Crops failed also because of swarms of locusts, usually in times of drought, and infestations of billions of caterpillars which followed times of heavy rain. Each caused enormous losses in grain; each led to horrific famines. The historic records are sketchy. 'Earthquake' is the connotation alongside 88 BC. 'Great drought' say the characters against the year 76 BC. 'Hailstones kill men' say the remarks of 66 BC. 'Great plague' is mentioned in 48 BC. But there are, too, signs of progress in the ancient scrolls. In 54 BC, state granaries were ordered built in the Yellow River region, a sure sign that crops were more than adequate, that the peasants who worked the land could put away excess produce to ensure survival in time of future famine. But the historical records on the whole make grim reading, and for the 2300 years in which the Huanghe's story

JAPAN BROADCASTING CORPORATION (NHK)

As the Huanghe flows to the sea, it creates hundreds of lakes and waterholes. Seen from the air, their crystal waters reflect the early morning sun.

YASUHIRO HAYASHI

*H*ydrologists, scientists and engineers study every kilometre of the river as it sweeps, wends and roars on its tempestuous course. Here, so far upstream that the waters are still clear and free of silt, a worker of the China Water Survey Committee takes a sampling of the stream. Chemicals and water content will be studied in an attempt to keep track of how the Huanghe changes on its long journey to the sea.

can be traced reliably, the entries make grim study. 30 BC: 'Great rains for over 40 days. Rumours being spread that a great flood would come. The people got into great confusion. Mountain slip. Earthquake.' Dynasties came and dynasties went, nobles rose in revolt, barbarian waves swept down from the north and west; the Yellow River rolled on, majestic, turbulent,unpredictable.

No matter the political priorities of emperors, the imperial court in every age had one concern that transcended all. From the birth of history, one of the most senior officials in the land had been in charge of water, his main responsibility the Huanghe. In 8 BC, the emperor called on engineers and wise men from throughout the realm to study the waters and devise ways by which they might be harnessed, by which the periodic disasters could be averted. There was much discussion. The planners reached consensus: the best way to avoid flooding was to lead the waters swiftly and directly to the sea, said their spokesman, the hydrologist Kia-jiang. A less favourable alternative was to divert the force of the river by canals. As a last resort, the Huanghe could be confined between high banks. These three methods of protecting the lowlands are basically the same as those being used today. But dykes could never be high enough; despite enormous labour the Yellow River burst out of its confining banks in 722 and spread 'like an inland sea' over the Shandong plains. It was nothing new; historical records show the dykes have been breached at least 1500 times in the past 2000 years. The tributaries have caused equal devastation as the main waterway.

Irrigation brought prosperity not only to peasants but also to kingdoms. The Chengkuo Canal opened in 246 BC is credited with laying the base for prosperity in the Chin Valley, bringing power to central Shanxi, making the area a vital economic zone and giving Qinshihuang the financial strength he needed to develop the military muscle he exercised to become emperor, found the Qin dynasty and unify China. About the same period, peasants in the fields in the Honei district in Henan sang as they worked their fields:

Yeh has a good administrator
His name is Shih
He opened the river Chang to irrigate Yeh
What used to be old alkali land can now grow rice and kaoling.

Few modern bureaucrats or politicians can count on such vocal, literally grassroots, support.

The people who live on the banks of the river have through the ages regarded the action of the waters as a reflection of the way in which the gods looked to their leaders. Rightly or wrongly, political fortunes have been tied closely to the rise and fall of the level of the Huanghe; regular flows have meant steady harvest, rising standards of living, prosperity and stability. Flood or droughts have meant famine, shortage, starvation and economic upheaval. When the people have been well fed, the rulers have slept peacefully. When the river brought bad fortune, wise emperors tried their best to placate the people.

Overleaf
Despite its savage and unpredictable changes of mood, the Huanghe has always been a vital artery for trade and communication. *Out at the River during the Spring Festival*, from the twelfth century AD, demonstrates the river's central role in public life.
BRITISH MUSEUM/NEWSWEEK

Copied in the twelfth or thirteenth century from a fourth century original attributed to Ki K'ai-chih, *The Nymph of the Lo* illustrates a poet's love affair with a river goddess — a bewitching creature capable of great tenderness and terrifying anger — who symbolised ancient China's preoccupation with her waterways.
FREER GALLERY/AMERICAN HERITAGE

SEIGO OTSUKA

Above and right

In celebrations that can be traced back to the time when northern Shaanxi was threatened by Huns, touring dance troupes bring flashes of colour to village life. Amid explosions of fireworks and beating of drums, the dancing girls in vivid silk perform exuberant steps. Local legends trace the dancing tradition to an age when women were expected to perform to encourage men to go and fight the invaders. These days, the aim is purely enjoyment. As part of the New Year celebrations, fires are lit in clay figures, casting a glow over village squares. The fires commemorate how the Han people showed border tribes how to dig coal out of the ground and use it for fuel.

There was constant striving by imperial courts in time of stability to bring succour to those in need. In 1529 there was a great famine in Henan, and a mandarin named Lin Hsi-yuan presented a detailed famine relief plan to the emperor. This called for several steps to be taken. First, aid workers had to be recruited whose urgent job was to survey the stricken area and find how many people were affected. Once the extent of the disaster was determined, victims should be graded into three levels of need. Grain should be given to the starving, money to the destitute and loans to the needy. Lin's program called for boiled rice to be distributed to the starving, medicine to the sick, soup to those on the way to recovery. The dead had to be buried, prisoners shown mercy, and birth control practised. The fiscal programs laid down by the Ming dynasty official were similar to those followed in many countries during the Great Depression that struck the western world exactly four centuries after the 1529 disaster in Henan; he urged government to lend money to buy and sell grain, to begin extensive public works to provide jobs and to lend cattle and seeds to promote economic growth. Speculation in grain and hoarding of rice were crimes to be punished with severity. Power along the Yellow River was always linked firmly with general prosperity, and rulers who wanted to keep their thrones endeavoured to ensure economic stability in the towns and full noodle bowls in the villages.

Never was politics so obviously bound to the life and livelihood of those who live along the river as in June 1938. For thousands of years there had been instances of the river and its tributaries being used as weapons of war. But never on this scale. The invading Imperial Japanese Army was smashing down through the North China Plain in the latest of the series of invasions which had begun in 1905 with the occupation of Taiwan and had been stepped up once again only six years earlier with the military occupation of Manchuria. The Nationalist armies of the Guomindang (much of their energies expended on fighting Chinese communists in the hinterland and pursuing the forces of Mao Zedong during the Long March of the Red Army) were seemingly helpless to fight the advancing Japanese to a stop. So it was decided to try to halt the enemy with the fearsome force of the Huanghe.

In June 1938, swollen by the summer downpours flooding down Shaanxi-Shanxi and the thaw melt from the Qinghai highlands, the river was running close to its brim when large numbers of Guomindang soldiers turned up at the hamlet of Huayangkou, a farming community nestled under the shadow of the dykes. The soldiers began to dig into the wall that held back the river. Explosive charges were inserted. Tunnels penetrated the earthworks put up over the centuries at so huge a cost in tears and sweat. The soldiers told the peasants to leave, that the dykes were being breached so the Yellow River could inundate the land and stop the invaders. Few of the farmers departed; they had no money, nowhere to go, nothing except the crops growing towards harvest in their fields and the humble possessions in

SEIGO OTSUKA

He tramped with the Long Marchers into the dreadful swamps of death of the Songpan Plain but Mr Zhang Xiao-jian was too ill to continue with the rest of the Red Army. Left behind, he married a Tibetan girl, raised a family, took to local ways. A half century after Mao Zedong and Zhu Deh continued on their way, he recalls the marching songs that helped keep him and a generation of young Chinese plodding on for the epic military adventure that changed the course of Asian history.

their homes. With a roar the dyke went up, the waters rushed out in a silty gush and swirled down through the breaches to the land lying below the level of the bed of the river, sweeping out over the plains. Nothing could stop the waters; ironically, nothing could stop the Japanese, either, and their advance continued as rapidly as that of the rising floodtides.

Nobody knows how many drowned. The waters rose, trapping some families in their homes. When water reached the rooftops, they tried to float away on scraps of furniture, makeshift rafts. Most died. But the greater toll was to come later. As many as 12.5 million were made homeless or forced to abandon the land to wander in search of food. Many stayed alive eating bark from sodden trees or wild herbs that had survived the inundation. The crops, of course, failed, stifled in the thick layer of silt laid down by the muddy waters. As far as scientists and historians have been able to tote up the final dreadful cost, at least 890 000 people died, their deaths attributable directly to the manmade calamity.

The helpless peasants, suffering pawns in the power plays of the mighty, would not forget the cause of their misfortune, and the writ of the Nationalists did not run long in the Henan-Shandong plain that had suffered in the deluge. After the Japanese surrender in 1945, during the brief truce in the civil war, the plain was under the titular control of the Nationalists. But active communist bands could count always on peasant support, and by the time the Eighth Route Army came storming down to bring communist rule to the area in 1948, substantial areas were already under control of Red units. It appeared, also, that Generalissimo Jiang Kaishek had learned little, if anything, from the earlier disastrous attempt to use the Yellow River as a weapon. As his regime tottered towards its end, Guomindang military planners once more plotted to breach the river, this time to stop the People's Liberation Army in its victorious advance. In far-off Yanan, many kilometres upstream on the Yan River tributary, communist master politician Zhou Enlai heard with horror of the scheme. A canny realist, the future premier of the People's Republic of China knew that the death and misery caused by the previous flood had brought Jiang Kaishek into deep opprobrium with some of his western supporters, especially among liberals in his major source of finance and weapons, the United States. The Guomindang were unlikely to be swayed by thoughts of what another inundation could mean to millions of helpless peasants, Zhou reasoned. But if their money and arms supplies from America were threatened, this could cause them to desist. So down from Yanan, Zhou dispatched one of the most remarkable men ever to have marched with the Red Army, the New York-born doctor, George Hatem. Known throughout China under his adopted name of Dr Ma Haide, he had helped treat the survivors of the Long March. Dr Ma went to Beijing, then Shanghai. In both places he spoke to foreign correspondents from all over the world who were in China covering the momentous events as the truce between the warring camps threatened to once more break down, exploding the twenty-year civil war towards a climax. Dr Ma patiently explained to the reporters what was planned, gave times and places and details of where the dykes were to be breached and recounted the horrific results of the 1938 flooding. Reporters questioned not only the Nationalist officials but also American advisers and politicians. Outrage mounted over the planned breach of the dykes for political purposes. Fearful of losing their supplies, worried about the international scandal which would erupt against them if history was repeated, the Guomindang forces retreated southwards leaving the Yellow River still confined.

Nature, more than man, has changed the course of the river. Above the town of Dongbatou in Henan province, the Huanghe has for the past five centuries kept to its course. Downstream, on the journey across the plain, matters have been different. In 1855, the river burst its dykes at Dongbatou and swung off on a new course. Over the ages, the mouth of the Yellow River has covered more than 1500 kilometres of coastline, occasionally disgorging its silt into the sea from Tianjin in the north or emptying further south through the Yangtze River, via the Huai valley. This area, covering 250 000 square kilometres (as large as all Japan) has seen the river make major changes in course no fewer than twenty-six times in the past 2000 years. Each one has spelt disaster for millions. As modern travellers today fly above the North China Plain, they can look down and, if the light is right, see through the haze the patterns on the land. These are like whorls in rich wood, curving patterns over the face of the fields of wheat and vegetables stretching to the horizon. The curls trace long-forgotten watercourses of the Huanghe.

SEIGO OTSUKA

Wallowing in backwash from turbulent currents, a ferry rolls wildly as oarsmen try to keep the boat upright in the water. Ferries come in all shapes, sizes and levels of sophistication, from simple sheepskin rafts to immense cable-drawn platforms.

追溯已往

RETRIEVING THE PAST

THE FIRST HAN civilisation arose on the banks of the Yellow River long before even China's recorded history begins, before the Iron Age, the Stone Age, the last ice age. Great cities rose, cultures flowered. On the banks of the river, pagodas, deep-carved visages of gods and crumbling walls of forgotten cities are vivid reminders of these vanished legacies. But a lot more treasure lies buried under deep layers of loess, hidden for a score of centuries from the people who came later. It is said that of all the major cities along the course of the river, the only one that is not built on the ruins of at least one earlier capital is Jinan, capital of Shandong. In Kaifeng, for example, the deeper archaeologists dig, the more they discover, the foundations of one civilisation built on the rooftops of one that went before. In some sites, six different ages stretching back more than 3400 years have been found in the one stack.

Throughout the length of the river, people are digging for the past. Every city, each province, has keen and dedicated archaeologists committed to searching for past glories hidden by the sands of time. They have found much; a lot remains undiscovered. Without doubt, Chinese social scientists lament, a great deal of the past has gone forever, never to be reclaimed.

This can partly be blamed on the geography of the heartland of the Chinese people – the capitals of Qin, Han, Sui, Tang, and other glorious dynasties were in the central course of the river where the land was formed over centuries by spreading tides of soft silt. They built their temples and memorials, their palaces and pleasure houses, of wood because granite and marble were unknown. Wood rots

Modelled with such vivacity that he seems ready to spring to his emperor's defence, this crossbowman was excavated in 1977. Traces of the figure's original colours can still be seen.

with history, burns when invaders sack a city, is destroyed by insects. The marble glories of ancient Greece were not created in China simply because there was no marble in the Yellow River valley. Instead, there was mud, lots of it, and clay. So was born ceramics in which much Chinese visual art reached its peak. And amid the deep loess that spread protective layers over dying civilisations, marvellous treasuries of ceramics remain to be discovered by a people seeking their cultural roots. The earthenware are more than just ornaments. They include jars, spoons, bowls and cooking pots, the necessities of everyday life. In these rich layers of soil can be traced the life of the common people.

So can the passing of kings. Of all the discoveries of the past ever made, none has excited scholar and layperson alike as much as the incredible lode of history which accidentally came to light near the ancient capital known as Chang'an, modern Xi'an. The only event comparable was the uncovering of the tomb of Egypt's King Tutankhamen. What was found at Xi'an was but the visible peak of a very large archaeological iceberg, most of which is still obscured by the earth that has preserved relics from the erosion of nature and the even more savage depredations of man. Man the creator can turn into man the destroyer; throughout China's saga plunderers, invaders, conquerors and usurpers have smashed and burned and pillaged the treasures they found. The motive has not always been joy in vandalism and quest for profit; often it is a wish to eradicate the glories of past rulers so that the endeavours of new regimes are not outshone by former achievements.

HIROYUKI USAMI

*I*n silent tribute to her deity, a clay hand servant stands ready to serve the Sacred Lady in the Jinci Temple of Shanxi. The huge complex near Taiyuan, capital of Shanxi, is one of the prime examples of religious architecture and statuary in China. The lady is believed to have been mother of Prince Shuyu of the Zhou dynasty, although the temple and its statues were not rebuilt until the Song era.

HIROYUKI USAMI

*H*eadless, battered by vandals but still standing vigilant guard, these courtiers and warriors confront visitors to the mausoleum of Chian Lin in the suburbs of Xi'an.

SEIGO OTSUKA

*L*ocal craftsmen fashioned this ornate and artistic ceiling of the local playhouse in the Song Dynasty. The decorative ceiling also covers an open-air forum where actors stage historical dramas.

Crafting a brick that will go into the edifice of a mosque, a Linxia brickmaker patiently follows ancient design. Wearing the distinctive white headgear of a Muslim, he is one of the big Hui minority scattered from Qinghai downriver as far as Henan.

Previous pages

The western Xia kings ruled a splendid realm, rich in both culture and cultivation, on the Great Bend near the present Hui region of Ningxia. Their moment on the stage of history ended when the Mongols swept forth, crushing the Xia kingdom as they destroyed so many other civilisations. Anthropologists puzzle still over the Xia written language and these lonely tombs raised in memory of ancient rulers.
TSUGUSATO OMURA

The preserved annals of the Han dynasty recount one such episode in AD 220 when the long period of Han rule was tottering in treachery and greed towards its tumultuous end. In 189, the emperor had died, and the brother of the empress called on a general named Tung Cho to put down an uprising of eunuchs. Instead of waging war for her, General Tung Cho grabbed the widowed empress and made off with her, along with her teenaged son who would be the new emperor. The general wanted to make his seven-year-old brother ruler of all China, so dethroned the legitimate boy emperor, killed the mother and placed his own brother on the Dragon Throne. During the resulting series of wars and campaigns, General Tung Cho abandoned Luoyang as the capital and moved with 'several millions of people' to Xi'an. Before he left, he put Luoyang to the torch, despoiling the graves of noble families and razing much of the city. His plundering troops did the rest, eradicating centuries of art and culture. Such was the fate of much of China's ancient glory.

The most recent wave of wanton rampagers who stamped into oblivion precious relics of Chinese culture were the lunatic Red Guards. During the dark decade of the Great Proletarian Cultural Revolution, millions of ardent but mindless youths did their best to wipe out what they scathingly called the Four Olds. They destroyed much, but the historical legacy of the past is so rich that even millions of chanting radicals could not eliminate it all. Indeed, much was safely hidden from the ardent armies with their scarlet armbands, just as it had been locked in the vaults of time from other profane savages; it was where it was safest, embraced by the deep loess earth of the North China Plain.

A decade ago, commune peasants digging a well stumbled on to an underground army. Rank upon rank of proud soldiers of the Qin dynasty were guarding their emperor, the ruler Qinshihuang. The warrior lord had died twenty-two centuries before, and to safeguard his passage and protect his tomb an army of terracotta warriors had been formed. For generations, local peasants and scholars alike had talked about the huge mound known locally as Mount Li. The dome, as tall as a fifteen-storey building, was widely believed to harbour relics of the past, but until the accidental discovery nobody had ever thought to probe deeply into its mysteries. Once the excited well-diggers climbed out of their excavation and proclaimed the wonders they had seen, the Central Government swiftly clamped a security cordon around the site to prevent robbers and curio seekers from destroying a vital chapter of China's heritage.

After ten years of toil, the army of the emperor, the first man to unify all of China as it was then known under one reign, is slowly being revealed. It is 8000 strong, a considerable force. Many comrades of those soldiers, servants and coachmen so far uncovered still stand watch beneath nearby banks of undisturbed earth. The Chinese archaeologists in charge of the dig, and their excited and envious foreign assistants invited from universities and museums all over the

GEORGE HOLTON/PHOTO RESEARCHERS INC

*N*ow protected by a gigantic hangar-like shelter, the earthenware army constructed to guard the tomb of the emperor Qinshihuang was damaged by rebel forces in 206BC.

GEORGE HOLTON/PHOTO RESEARCHERS INC

*P*ainstaking excavation work has continued since the first soldiers were discovered in 1974, when local farmers drilling wells in search of water found instead fragments of pottery figures.

Right

*A*lthough the thousands of pottery guardians were fabricated on a mass-production basis, the artistry of their design is evident in the naturalism of this unarmoured crossbowman.

world, are taking things very slowly and very cautiously. After 2200 years, the army of the emperor is in no hurry. Western experts are full of praise for the systematic way in which Chinese scholars are proceeding with the patient excavation and delighted with the museum that houses those relics, commonly described as the best of its type on earth.

Chinese, no matter their political persuasion, are intensely proud of their sweeping cultural heritage and peasant farmer and learned professor alike feel a strong bond between themselves and the civilisations that went before. They are linked, Emperor Qinshihuang and the men who plough the fields alongside his slowly uncovering tomb. Long-dead conqueror and modern peasant are at either end of a continuous civilisation. The pottery soldiers, part of China's heritage, are common to both.

It did not always stand undisturbed, this faithful army of the dead. Only four years after the emperor's death, wayward soldiers of the succeeding dynasty, the Han, plundered his grave. But for many centuries past the Xi'an army stood undisturbed as history turbulently marched by the hidden secrets of Mount Li.

SETH JOEL/WHEELER PICTURES

Protected by his armour, a charioteer stands poised to charge *(above)*; an officer, discovered at the head of a column of soldiers *(right)*.

Previous pages

A cavalryman and his mount, unearthed together in 1977.

SETH JOEL/WHEELER PICTURES

SETH JOEL/WHEELER PICTURES

*D*espite their numbers, the emperor's guardians are modelled with astonishing detail; this kneeling crossbowman provided archaeologists with a rare insight into styles of dress and ornate hairstyles.

Right

A three-legged *chueh*, or vessel for heating wine, cast in bronze in the thirteenth or twelfth century BC. Its overall shape is an obvious development from much older pottery objects that can be dated from perhaps as long as 7000 years ago.

The site of the tomb and its attendant army was well documented at the time of the burial of Emperor Qinshihuang. Writing a century after the event, the Han dynasty historian Chien Ssu-ma recorded that the emperor had begun work on his last resting place while still filled with vigorous life.

> As soon as the First Emperor became King of Qin, excavations and buildings had been started at Mount Li. After he won the empire more than 700 000 conscripts from all parts of the country worked there. They dug through three underground streams and poured molten copper for the outer coffin, and the tomb was filled with models of palaces, pavilions and offices as well as fine vessels, precious stones and rarities. All the country's streams, the Yellow River and the Yangtze, were reproduced in quicksilver and by some mechanical means made to flow into a miniature ocean. The stars shone above and the regions of the earth were laid out below.

To guard this vast treasure, cunning artisans rigged series of drawn crossbows with hidden triggers designed to impale intruders into the realm of the dead. But such devices did not deter plunderers.

Some archaeologists believe the terracotta figures, each one brilliantly individual, were fashioned by court artists on real members of the royal entourage. They also suspect the army may be but one of four buried formations that accompanied Qinshihuang on his last journey. Chinese architecture and design has always aimed at balance, at bringing order and symmetry to things. The buried army was found 1500 metres due east of the mound where the emperor was buried. There is speculation that more warriors, courtiers, workers, concubines and other figures could be still standing watch in similar underground barracks to the north, west and south, vast cultural treasures still to be located.

Many experts theorise that the figures found at Xi'an were sculpted so truly simply because no living slaves would be entombed with the ruler, as had been the practice in earlier dynasties when kings were generally accompanied to the grave by warriors, women, servants and horses, all buried alive. But the respected German missionary-scholar Dr Ernst Faber, in his massive and masterly *History of China* published posthumously in 1902, claimed that Qinshihuang was accompanied to the afterlife by more than stone and clay figures. After the great unifier died in 209 BC, his son, Erh-shih, built a mausoleum to his father. It was described as a huge underground palace ornamented with immense treasures of gold and jewels. Several hundred young concubines, selected for their beauty, were forced into the tomb, known as the Spirit City of Qinshihuang, before it was sealed. If so, their bones may be found amid the jade and gold when archaeologists finally open the inner sanctum of the man who united China.

Whatever the cause of the irregular wanderings of the seat of government, it seems certain that along 1000 kilometres of valley from Shaanxi to the coast there

*C*onstant, elaborate and sometimes almost obsessive ritual lay at the heart of the Shang dynasty, and even such decorative pieces as this *tsun* vase took on a religious meaning far removed from their original purposes.

FREER GALLERY/LAURIE PLATT WINFREY INC

*O*ne of the most engaging Chinese art discoveries of the nineteenth century was the unearthing of this bronze eleventh century BC rhinoceros. Remarkably accurate in its form and details, it attests to a sophisticated knowledge of anatomy and biology.

BRUNDAGE COLLECTION/LAURIE PLATT WINFREY INC

SEIGO OTSUKA

*T*he confidence and mastery of form that are evident in Qinshihuang's entombed warriors can be seen in the harmonious proportions of an earthenware vessel, itself recalling the legacy of Chinese Bronze Age art.

FREER GALLERY/LAURIE PLATT WINFREY INC

A richly decorated elephant of the *huo* type illustrates early Chinese artisans' familiarity with the world; perhaps scholars or pilgrims brought the first descriptions of such fabulous beasts back to the Imperial court.

*H*eavy and sustaining, the big bread rolls of wheat are the basis for everyday meals in the North China Plains. Rice here is a luxury, rare to most people. It is *man-tou*, steamed bread buns, that accompany every meal, or hearty noodle dishes made from the same enriching flour. Where the land will not yield wheat, millet or barley grows. Scientists, examining grains found in excavations dating before the start of the historical era, believe the first cultured grain was a seed-like millet.

Overleaf

*F*lower Mountain in Shaanxi is one of China's sacred peaks. To climb to the top of the 2200-metre summit is a tiring expedition but the view is said to improve the health.
HIROYUKI USAMI

are buried the remains of dozens of cities that hold clues to a lost past. But after thirty-five centuries, how deep do they lie under their shrouds of earth? Since the Xia and Shang ruled, floods of the Huanghe and ceaseless settlement of loess from the skies have built up formidable layers of new earth over the relics of China's remote past. Many of the seats of early power, now little more than a dim memory inscribed in the oldest of historical records, will never be found.

What has been found is so stupendous that it would take archaeologists, anthropologists and historians many years to absorb. In Xi'an, alone, there are eleven known tombs of emperors of the Western Han and eighteen of the Tang. The sites of graves of concubines and courtiers, chancellors and generals are also known. Some are believed to be intact, the contents untouched. On the outskirts of Luoyang, ranks of stone elephants, winged horses and proud soldiers stand erect on a loess outcrop guarding the tombs of seven Song emperors. Five of these are believed to have escaped the clutches of ten centuries of thieves.

National pride in the past has placed excavation of the treasures of the dynasties firmly in the hands of the government in Beijing. Officials supervise every excavation, give permission for each dig. Despite this, there has been considerable evidence that the past is still being plundered. Ignoring strictly enforced laws which carry heavy penalties that ban the export of relics, the opening of China to the outside world of tourism has helped accelerate an international demand for ancient porcelain and statues. This demand is met by middlemen, mainly Overseas Chinese, who tour China with the aim of buying up old curios to sell at a huge profit abroad. They are aided by peasants who live near tombs and find the temptation of high prices irresistible. In some stretches of the Great Wall, greed has succeeded where generations of barbarians failed; huge gaps in the Wall mark spots where local farmers have knocked out stones to break them into fist-sized mementoes. Thoughtless tourists carry these away to boast that they have a bit of China's heritage at home.

Much has been unearthed dating from long before the earliest emperor mounted the Dragon Throne. Discoveries on the North China Plain in Hebei province, where the Yellow River has meandered on many of its courses to the sea, prove that cereals were cultivated there at least 8000 years ago. In Shaanxi, cultivated millet has been dated as being planted 6000 years ago. As far upriver as Gansu and Qinghai, millet grains have been dated back to the New Stone Age, and in Jiangsu and Shandong around old estuaries of the river there is equal proof of early settled farming. Stone sickles and mills for crushing grain and ploughshares made of bone have been found in Henan. So have iron ploughshares designed to be drawn by oxen. The importance of agriculture as the base of China's early economy is driven home by discoveries such as a sophisticated harrow drill, combining ploughing and sowing, invented in the Han dynasty. Its like is still in use today. Air

HIROYUKI USAMI

Armies have tramped back and forth over the troubled soil of Shanxi since long before the first dynasty arose. Surprisingly, much remains of historical and cultural value. The temple monastery of Xianzhingsi, west of Pingyao, is a fine example of religious architecture.

fans to winnow grain, water-powered mills to crush it into flour; examples of inventions have recently been unearthed in Henan and dated 1000 years earlier than similar discoveries first appeared in Europe.

These finds reinforce earlier theories that stable agricultural societies flourished at an extremely early stage in human history along the entire length of the Huanghe. And they prove once again the lessons taught in schools today and in the classics of Confucius: throughout the long history of humankind on the North China Plain, prosperity and development have rested always on the toil of the farmer. In turn, the farmer's crops have depended on the rich soil of the plains and the waters of the Yellow River.

Left

Scientists and anthropologists trace back the cultivation of millet in the Huanghe valley for tens of thousands of years. The grain has been found in excavations of early agriculturalists who ploughed the ochre soil long before the misty beginnings of the Xia dynasty. Methods of sorting the grain from the chaff have changed little. Farmers a hundred centuries ago probably threw their harvest into the air, allowed wind to carry away the straw and caught the heavier grain in a woven basket.

SEIGO OTSUKA

In museums throughout the length of the river, particularly in the historic heartland provinces, there are fine collections of the treasures of the past. The Bronze Age came early to China, flowered for centuries, leaving behind a legacy that can still today inspire young artists.

降伏蛟龍

TAMING THE DRAGON

THE HUANGHE ROSE rapidly in Qihe county, Shandong, during the big flood of August 1958. August is a month traditionally associated with disaster along the lower reach of the river; many of the most horrendous inundations of history have taken place in the seventh moon of the lunar calendar. Along the dykes on either side of the river as it swept in turgid rage down through Henan and Shandong, more than two million men and women stood flood-watch duty. The flood peak was passing through Qihe on its way to the safety of the Gulf of Bohai when two schoolboys ran urgently towards a 'rush squad', a group of local men stationed on the embankment ready to dash to any potential trouble spot. The boys had seen one, an area where water was seeping openly through the side of the levee. Having grown up alongside the river, they realised swiftly the danger. Once water makes its way through a dyke it quickly eats away at the interior, and within minutes a gentle flow can become a gushing jet pushed out by the tremendous pressure of the angry, brimming river. Fortunately the emergency team got there in time, staunched the flow, averted the danger. The swift action of the two young schoolboys possibly stopped a major breach in the dyke. But they were only following instructions given in their classroom because everyone along the banks of the Yellow River knows the basic lessons of flood control.

Just as the two boys in 1958 knew of the danger of water coming through the dyke, so do scores of millions of people who live today along the river and its tributaries. Constant public education programs ensure that the hard lessons of the past are not forgotten. Films of vast floods are shown regularly on television,

*B*oiling in muddy fury, trapped waters of the Huanghe churn furiously through the outlets of Chingtonxia dam.

SEIGO OTSUKA

*E*roded by water, cut by winds, cliffs outside Xining frame two young shepherds.

and elders are encouraged to tell the young generation of days a half-century ago when people starved to death, families sold their children, entire villages perished because of flood or famine. The education drive is just part of the mass organisation effort that keeps communities along the river ever on the alert.

In the modern era as in centuries past the main challenge posed by the river has been its tumultuous floods. Controlling the ferocity of the waters at their peak remains the major concern of those responsible for the safety of the North China Plain. To keep the Huanghe within its boundaries, twin sets of dykes stretch for hundreds of kilometres along either side of its lower reaches as it heads for the Gulf of Bohai. These dykes are wonders of modern engineering, more powerful, more impressive now than ever in history. They need to be; continuing deposits of silt in the riverbed have raised the level more than 2 metres in the past twenty years. The river is continually building itself higher, and the people must keep raising the level of the constraining walls just to keep pace.

The dykes of the past were gigantic earthworks thrown up at incredible cost and effort. Today, they are no less costly but a lot more sophisticated and efficient, using every technique perfected by hydraulic engineers and scientists. The dykes run along both banks of the lower river, a length of 1400 kilometres, not including the embankments that stretch up the major tributaries and the secondary lines of defence that run parallel to the main barriers. Today's structures are built basically on top of older lines of defence, but in the past thirty years have been significantly strengthened in three major periods of reconstruction.

Upkeep and maintenance work is constant; work teams patrol the embankments daily looking for weaknesses. At periods of high water, volunteers from local communities closely examine the sloping outward faces of the barriers, and any damp spots are noted. Later, repair teams will visit and probe the bank with special equipment developed by Yellow River Commission engineers, a machine that looks rather like a small tank without armour. This uses a long steel probe to penetrate the concrete and rock of the outer skin into the packed earth of the older, inner core of the dykes. If a cavity is found, a thick-setting concrete mixture is pumped under pressure down through the probe to fill the interior of the embankment with a granite-hard mixture. The work is endless; statistics over the past thirty years show no fewer than 92 million probes were made into the dykes on the lower reaches, and concrete grouting was pumped into 330 000 hidden defects.

As the cores of the dykes were being toughened, so the outer walls were being expanded constantly. As well as being high enough to prevent rising waters from coming over the top of the barriers, the embankments must be wide and strong enough to contain the enormous weight of the elevated river when it is full of water. With a watercourse 8 kilometres wide full to the brim of rushing, silt-clogged water, pressure against the dykes is a huge burden. The barriers must be strong to

HIROYUKI USAMI

*C*onstant vigilance is the price of safety. Along the North China Plain as the Huanghe flows through Henan and Shandong hundreds of thousands of people stand ready to fight threats of flooding. They come from all walks of life — office workers from the great cities as well as village farmers — united by the knowledge that once the banks are broken, the vengeful water will sweep all before it on the low plains. These burly Shandong men leap to the defence to repair a wall of a dyke deliberately breached to enable 'rush teams' to practise.

SEIGO OTSUKA

*F*rom the high plateau of Qinghai through its long journey down to the Gulf of Bohai, the Huanghe provides a living faucet for farmers. Scientists estimate that more than half the total water in the river is drawn off for irrigation. This deep canal in Qinghai takes water to the fields of the minority Sala nationality near Xining.

Previous pages

*T*win jewels of the headwaters, the lakes of Ngoring and Gyaring are legendary sources of the Huanghe. In Tibetan and Han lore alike, it was thought the Yellow River rose from the linked lakes before starting its journey over the Qinghai plateau. People of many ages have marvelled at the beauty of the twin lakes, connected by a ten-kilometre stretch of river where the waters run between the rolling plains of the Qinghai plateau.
YASUHIRO HAYASHI

bear the strain. They are. China has limitless manpower resources and it has been traditionally on these that the eternal fight to harness the river has rested. So it was in the early years of communist rule. Just as emperors 3000 years before had made flood control a central concern, so the new regime in Beijing made conquest of the Yellow River a matter of priority, a vital part of state policy.

The foundations of the old dykes were mostly sandy or clay soils, and the busy water could easily undermine them. This historically has caused as many dyke breaches as waters coming over the top of barriers, and making the lower parts of the embankment as broad as possible is a basic design concept for engineers of levees. On the flat plain of Henan and Shandong, material to build strong barricades is not easily found. So the first methods of strengthening the dykes after 1949 were basically the same as had been used for thousands of years: the accumulated silt was scooped from the bed of the Yellow River by armies of impressed workers and stamped on to the slopes of the broadening embankment.

This manual method of adding to the thickness of the walls is now a thing of the past. Fleets of specially designed and constructed suction dredges now prowl the waters close to the edges of the river, pumping silt-rich water through thick umbilical pipes leading on to the banks. When the water evaporates, solid layers of sediment are left behind, adding to the weight, thickness – and strength – of the dykes. As a bonus, the water spillage helps farmers to irrigate and fertilise their fields, and it reduces the load of silt in the river bed. The silt pumped outside the dykes settles into earth; over thirty years it has filled in low, swampy land formerly too salty or alkaline to farm, making 200 000 hectares of new arable land. From 1949 to 1979, engineers using this method had added more than 160 million cubic metres of earthworks to 245 kilometres of dykes.

But skill as well as sheer massive strength is needed to control the waters, and while the barriers have been continually widened and raised the embankments fronting the river have become more complex. The twin aim of these works, which stretch hundreds of kilometres on either side of the river, is to protect the vulnerable flanks of the levees and control the flow of the Huanghe. The easiest way to prevent water action from undermining the barricades and threatening the safety of the dykes is to use a method perfected thousands of years ago, to roll willow branches into long coils around stones and sink them at the base of the embankment. Silt swiftly forms around such simple groynes, covers them with a layer of sediment and adds another cover of safety.

Modern methods are more effective albeit much more expensive. Engineers have devised special effects to train the waters to act the way they want. This is done by special construction works aimed at getting the water to flow in the least harmful manner. Most of these are in the form of small concrete spur dykes which divert the flow of water away from the main embankments and out into the central

HIROYUKI USAMI

*D*ramatic scenery lines the banks of the swiftly flowing river as the Huanghe pours downstream from the dam in the Linxia Gorge.

*D*ownstream from the Liuchiaxia dam, the Yellow River cuts through the gorge.

Previous pages

*W*hen engineers complete work on the huge dam planned to block the flow of the Huanghe at Dragon Sheep Canyon, near Xining, the artificial lake will spread many kilometres upstream.
HIROYUKI USAMI

river channel. More than 5000 of these, most of them 10 to 30 metres in length, protrude from the dyke walls out into the riverbed. They are laid at an angle pointing downstream and into the middle of the river. Instead of the waters in flood scouring the base of the main dykes, a major cause of breaches in bygone years, the new engineering techniques turn the force of the deluge back into the middle of the river channel.

Officials of the Yellow River Conservancy Commission are confident that even if the Huanghe reaches high flood levels of 22 000 million cubic metres per second, the present dykes would safely hold the waters. But they are designing safety margins for unforeseen deluges as bad as any in history. Time and again along thousands of kilometres of its course,the river is halted by a series of huge dams and reservoirs. These are safety valves built into the river to prevent floods and to relieve droughts.

The dams on the Huanghe and its tributaries are also designed to provide a source of electric power, but the overriding consideration in their construction was always flood relief. The key reservoir is at Sanmenxia (Three Gate Gorge) in Henan province, a project conceived in the heady days of the 1950s when much of the youth of China was imbued with revolutionary fervour and convinced that, given the will, any deed was possible. Planners hoped, with one bold move, to tame the river in a stroke. They chose the turbulent narrows of the gorge as the best place to strike. At first with the aid of Russian advisers, then after the break with the Soviet Union, by themselves, Chinese engineers plugged the river with a gigantic concrete barrage. Trouble soon became apparent. Planners realised that when the waters swept down from loess hills they were heavy with silt. But it was thought much of the silt would run through the turbines that turned the electricity generators (it didn't, they clogged) and more sediment would escape through overflow channels. The calculations were sadly astray, engineers now concede. The heavy sediment swiftly settled to the bottom of the mighty artificial lake, and the waters began to choke on their own mud.

In 1960,the reservoir behind Sanmenxia dam held 96.2 billion cubic metres of water. Two years later, so much silt had collected on the bottom of the placid water that there was only room for 81.2 billion cubic metres. By 1964, deposits of sediment had grown so large that the lake contained only 56.6 billion cubic metres of water. Frantic redevelopment plans were made, and reconstruction of the dam included special underwater escape tunnels designed to carry away silt-laden waters far downstream. Hopes for massive electrification were abandoned. Installed generating capacity was 900 000 kilowatts; maximum potential is now 250 000. The generators were scrapped, sacrificed to get rid of clogging silt. Today, the reservoir contains but 7 billion cubic metres of water; the rest of the lake is thick layers of silt.

SEIGO OTSUKA

*I*t was thought that the great dam at Sanmenxia in Henan would solve many of the problems of power, flooding and irrigation along a significant section of the Huanghe. But scientists, engineers and hydrologists had to revise their ambitious hopes when waters began to rise behind the concrete embankment. Silt settled far faster than anticipated, cutting down the water capacity in the artificial lake, drastically reducing the expected amount of generating power and making the enormous work an embarrassment rather than an asset.

HIROYUKI USAMI

The lake behind the Liuchiaxia dam backs up for many kilometres, providing one of the most significant reservoirs along the entire Huanghe.

Still, Sanmenxia and the other dams on the Huanghe and tributaries provide important safety precautions. Above the Three Gate Gorge lies 92 per cent of the entire catchment area of the river including the most dangerous areas where summer downpours can cause instant flash floods to go cascading downstream to hit the plains. In dry seasons, water is stored. In times of threat of flood, the discharge can be regulated to help control the height of the river many kilometres downstream. Planners say that if there is a deluge upstream, the dam can hold back the outflow to a maximum of 15 000 cubic metres a second. If the rains fall below the dam and the situation is serious, the discharge gates can be shut, holding back about 3.5 billion cubic metres.

Despite all these precautions, river planners still look for worst-case scenarios which will stretch their impressive engineering works to maximum. In addition to huge dykes, improved channelling, water retention dams and anti-erosion programs, there is another important strategy in their planning. If flood levels reach critical heights, the hundreds of sluice gates along the river can be raised allowing a significant percentage of the water to escape from between the main dykes to

HIROYUKI USAMI

Spanning the Huanghe at Linxia, a graceful arched bridge is one of many new crossings which in recent years have been thrown over the turbulent waters.

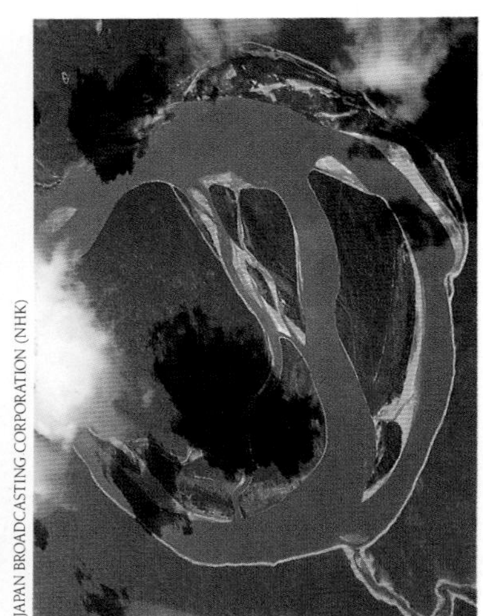
JAPAN BROADCASTING CORPORATION (NHK)

*I*n a giant ox-bow, the river turns upon itself to make another of its countless changes of course. Passing through the warm, moist fringes of subtropical Sichuan province, the land around the river is unusually verdant.

flow safely out into the irrigation canals. In addition, two huge detention basins on either bank of the Huanghe have been readied to cope with what hydrologists term 'extraordinary large floods' which could one day occur. Everybody hopes such a deluge will not come; engineers have planned for it if it should.

The diversion basins are enormous. If the river should reach levels where it looks likely to burst the banks, huge amounts of water can be safely run off into the basins at Dongpinhu and Jindi. Between them, they cover 2948 square kilometres and can contain 40 billion cubic metres of floodwaters. More than 200 kilometres of dykes up to 13 metres high surround the basins. Inside the dykes, living under the threat of inundation should the historic deluge ever come, are more than 1.5 million people. Their homes have been built on raised platforms of earth, and elevated roads run across the floor of the basin to take them to safety if the basin is ever flooded.

Just as the inhabitants in the man-made diversion basins stand ready to flee if the waters are released into their low-lying farmlands, so do millions of peasant farmers along the entire lower course of the Huanghe stand eternally vigilant as part of an army to combat the threat of natural flood. This home guard lives with a battlecry that has been handed down for many generations: 'Dykes are of no value without people to care for them.'

The organisation of the peasants to fight rising waters and to cope with potential disaster is as impressive an achievement as the hundreds of kilometres of dykes that in normal times protect their homes from the Yellow River. Allied with the hundreds of hydrometric survey measuring stations along the river, the peasant army is organised in every village, each town, all production brigades and communities and cities down through Shaanxi, Shanxi, Henan and Shandong. It is a complex but commonsense organisation, from the highest levels of the Central Government through provincial capitals and the Yellow River Commission reaching down to a farmer in a remote village.

The command posts are in major towns along the river where the flood crest threatens. As waters rise, the warnings go out, broadcast over the public loudspeakers in every village. They call the peasants to the alert, sound loudly the alarm that the ancient enemy is once more on the rise. Much encouragement is given to recruit to the army of flood fighters not only the rural peasants but also people from other walks of life: the army, miners, students, city clerks and factory workers are all urged to take part. The governors of the four provinces and the director of the Yellow River Commission are at the head of regional flood protection command posts. Stress is on planning for the worst calamity that can be foreseen so that what passes for a normal disaster along the river can be handled more easily. Flood protection precautions are part of daily life, coordinated by local government officials as part of their normal work. The main emphasis is on dyke

TSUGUSATO OMURA

*E*ngineers of the Han era built this irrigation canal at Zhongwei when the Ordos first came under Chinese rule 2000 years ago. It works still, bringing life and prosperity to farmers on the Ordos plateau.

maintenance and observance. If anyone sees a weak spot, an animal burrow (foxes and badgers cause many problems) or an area of dampness, it is their task to report it to local cadres who will call on the nearest work team to remedy the fault.

Staff at the Yellow River Commission are practical engineers, not hopeful idealists. They deal with problems they can plainly see: rising river levels, increasing silting of the bed, the dangers of the 'worst-possible-case' scenario that would see a horrific, unprecedented 55 000 cubic metre flood that would test to the limit every device, every precaution, every safety feature that they have built into the banks of the Huanghe during the past forty years. Not for many years has the Yellow River lived up to its awesome reputation of being China's Sorrow. One day, its flow measured by checks and balances of man against the unpredictable surge and bullying of nature, the Huanghe might be renamed, may rejoice in the title of China's Pride. But not yet, say engineers of the Yellow River Commission. There is a long way to go yet. The Yellow River, they warn, is still not tamed.

Left

Sullen and running heavy after recent rains, a tributary of the Huanghe runs swiftly under a suspended footbridge, a recent addition that has made life easier for farmers.

Overleaf

When winter brings frigid northern winds blowing down from Siberia and Mongol steppes, the Huanghe turns into an icy highway. No ferries are needed on this stretch of the river between Shanxi and Shaanxi when nature provides a bridge of ice.

SEIGO OTSUKA

TSUGUSATO OMURA

A gleam in the setting sun, the Huanghe slides peacefully through Ningxia province.

东流の海

From the Heartland to the Sea

Tourists standing on the impressive road bridge that spans the Yellow River on the fringes of Shandong's capital city of Jinan can look down and, if they are lucky, occasionally see one of the legendary, allegedly lucky, carp of the river leap from the water. Any peasant tending the fields of sweet corn, green beans and dark purple aubergines in the temporary fields between the wide-set levees will be glad to tell the visitor that the fish are jumping from the water to get a breath of air. There is too much silt in the water to allow fish to use their gills, the farmers will patiently explain. There is some truth in this old wives' tale; the Yellow River provides remarkably little in the way of aquatic life, far less than the generous bounties given up by the Yangtze, the Pearl or thousands of lesser streams.

Apart from junks and a few small river boats, the river is not navigable in its lower stretch. It does not yield fish. In times past, it regularly flooded and brought death and misery to millions, and today the Central Government in Beijing spends many millions of *yuan* and employs an army of people to control the waters. But despite the lack of useful and attractive attributes, disregarding the expense and dangers, the people of Shandong bear a deep regard for the muddy torrent which over the centuries has dropped rich layers of silt and helped to build their land.

The closer the river gets to its rendezvous with the sea, the richer are the people who live by its banks. Shandong is one of the wealthiest provinces in all China. Much of this richness is due directly to the benefits bestowed by the great river that for its final 617 kilometres bisects much of its fertile plains.

Suspended by huge steel cables, the bridge at Jinan is the longest crossing over the Huanghe and the one closest to the mouth. Across it rolls the wealth of Shandong province, much of it still pulled by hundreds of donkey carts.

*B*oys at Anyang. Excavations here have unearthed a royal palace, tombs, houses and workshops from the Shang dynasty. The tombs contained thousands of bones inscribed with the earliest known Chinese writing.

The hilly Shandong Peninsula juts aggressively out into the Yellow Sea like the head of some enormous lizard. Until 1853 the Huanghe ran well south of this huge promontory, but in the great deluge of that year the river broke its banks and abruptly changed course. In ages past the waters have sought the sea on either side of the peninsula.

Statistics carefully kept by provincial officials show that the Huanghe has an unhappy penchant of flowing over its dykes on grim average of twice every three years. In the eighty-three years between 1855 and 1938, there were no fewer than fifty-seven overflows in the lower courses of the river. These were times of even more sanguinary oppression than usual for the long-suffering peasants of the North China plains; in addition to the customary desolation caused by excesses of nature there were warlords, revolution, invasion, rampant banditry, the collapse of empire, foreign incursion and occupation and civil war. There was also the frightful Henan famine of 1943–44 in which at least three million starved to death.

In autumn and winter, when the flow is at its lowest, the Huanghe in Shandong is not a vastly impressive sight. Indeed, so much water is taken off upstream for irrigation that at the end of the dry season in a particularly arid year it is possible to walk across the riverbed and watch the children splashing thigh-deep through the thick and turgid pools. But in July and August, after the thaw 5000 kilometres upstream has melted snow and ice, and with summer downpours in Shaanxi and Shanxi adding enormous contributions to the flood, the river is full, sometimes running brim to brim between the riverbank dams. The contrary nature of the river is one of extremes; the historical pattern is of scorching droughts that leave the land dry and parched, followed by enormous cloudbursts. The dramatic rains hitting the concrete-hard fields cannot soak into the earth, and in the frantic runoffs that follow the river rises. This is what happened in the tremendous floods of 1899 which submerged the entire Shandong plain.

The water table beneath the city of Jinan was once so high that the provincial capital was known as the City of Springs. The big Batou Spring which once gurgled impressively in the centre of the town is now considerably lower and the outflow appreciably decreased. But provincial agricultural officials are undismayed by this comparative waning of the springs of Jinan; if the water table is too high, it can lead to fields getting too alkaline. Better a field of golden wheat than a spring of water, say the farmers.

Shandong, straddling the coast between Beijing and Shanghai, prides itself on having the best of both places, the classical culture of the capital and the cosmopolitan outlook of the great port-city on the Yangtze. It also boasts of its own unique attractions. Not least of these are the intellectual pretensions that come from being birthplace of both Confucius and Mencius.

After years of trying to politely ignore Confucius and destruction of his family

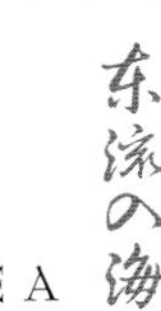

HIROYUKI USAMI

*B*athed with the light of early morning, farmers carry loads of precious nightsoil from their village to their fields along the valley of the Fen. Despite great advances in agriculture, organic fertiliser still plays an important role in keeping fertile the good earth of the Yellow River valley.

*T*he sculpted columns of the main building of the Temple of Confucius, Qufu. Once protected as a holy site, Qufu was partially desecrated during the Cultural Revolution; only recently has it again become a place of pilgrimage.

cemetery and criticism of his teachings during the Cultural Revolution, the communist regime has come to a somewhat uneasy truce with the long-departed sage. His home town of Qufu is now being promoted actively as a tourist destination, and the clan mansion, a temple and the forest in which he and relatives are buried are now descended upon regularly by foreign visitors as well as Chinese. Through the long roll of dynasties, emperors came here to award posthumous honours to China's greatest teacher and to pay tribute to a man who left for his legacy a code of conduct adhered to still. These days, those who come to admire the sculptures and to trot through the forested park on re-created carriages of a former age are as likely to come from Manchester, Manhattan or Melbourne as from Manchuria.

Provincial tourism authorities now plan to make the bridge the focal point for a hugely ambitious plan to re-create an entire Song dynasty city in the middle of Kaifeng, long the capital of the Song emperors. If necessary permission and finances are received from the Central Government in Beijing, city planners anticipate the day when tourists will be floated through a series of canals linking city lakes to sights such as the Iron Pagoda, the stately Dragon Hall and sprawling Xiangguo Temple. During the prosperous Song age, more than 10 000 traders and craftsmen were said to have set up regular shop around the temple. Plans are for their descendants to return; under schemes to develop Kaifeng as a tourist centre to rival Xi'an, artists and artisans practising their crafts with ancient methods and equipment will operate along the canals and in the temples and shrines. The aim is to create, with modern comforts, a Kaifeng as much as possible as it was in the age of the Song.

Their rule ended in Henan in 1127 when the fierce Jurchen barbarians invaded, plundered and pillaged northern China. They put the capital, Luoyang, to the torch. The Song emperor was captured, and another took his place, leading the reign south to escape the barbarians. This was a significant step because over the preceding centuries the Chinese people had been emigrating away from the ancestral homelands along the Huanghe. Now the emperor was following his mobile and adventurous people. For the first time, political power moved from the banks of the Yellow River and shifted to the Yangtze valley and the new court at Hangzhou. This was to give, for the first time, recognition to the economic power being developed in what had in earlier times been wild jungle area occupied by primitive tribes. Once cleared, the Yangtze's fertile, well-watered soil was found perfect for rice cultivation. But neither the Song in Hangzhou nor the Jurchen in Henan were to last much longer on the stage of history because an even more ferocious newcomer, the Mongol, was soon to arrive and snatch all power in China in bloodstained hands. The Mongols, too, moved the capital of the newly conquered nation away from the Huanghe heartland, this time to the city they called Dadu which later became known as Peking and then as Beijing.

Right

*D*eep in meditation, an elderly monk contemplates a life dedicated to a vigorous path toward righteousness. A priest at the famed monastery at Shaolin, he is a man of action as well as deep thought. It was here, in the shrouded mountains of Henan, that monks developed martial arts that gave wandering and unarmed holy men protection against bandits in dangerous days. From the Shaolin monastery the message of the holy men spread wide, as far as Japan where it formed the seeds that led to the Zen arm of Buddhism.

YASUHIRO HAYASHI

Elaborate and dignified, this statue of Confucius at the sage's mausoleum in Qufu is now a popular regional tourist destination.

The Songs were the last Chinese rulers to hold sway over China from a capital on the Yellow River. With them, imperial power departed forever from the banks of the waterway on which the Chinese legacy began. But behind them they left a glorious heritage still visible today.

So did many others. For a variety of reasons, mostly financial, Henan has in the years since China reopened its doors been widely ignored by the tourist rush. The normal track of foreign visitors sweeps from Shanghai and Beijing over Henan to Xi'an. Airports in the province are few and are anyway unable to handle the new generation of jumbo jets. Hotels and other facilities are few. In recent years, Henan has played host to a meagre 40 000 foreign visitors a year, a stunningly small number. But at the same time, internal Chinese tourism is booming. About 12 million people from other provinces go there every year to wonder at the ancient monuments and cities from which their cultural heritage sprang.

In AD 495 at the time of the Northern Wei dynasty, a sect of Buddhist monks began work on a monastery. Forbidden by the precepts of their faith to carry weapons, the monks needed some form of protection to guard against the roaming warrior bands that infested the land. They found the answer in physical fitness and self-defence. Today, the monks of Shaolin are still schooled in the disciplines of their martial arts, the most famous form of self-defence of all the schools in China. It is a popular venue for western visitors who follow the mental and physical strictures of the teachings of the meek warrior monks of Shaolin. Temples abound in Henan, witness to the long history of faiths in the province. The White Horse monastery outside Luoyang was built in AD 68, the first to be erected after the introduction of Buddhism to China from India. Much has been destroyed over the years. That which remains, like the splendid Attic of the Goddess of Mercy, gives glimpses into the past. There are plans by the provincial government to restore much of the ancient glory of Henan, things like the oldest observatory in China, built during the Yuan dynasty so scholars could study the heavens.

Overleaf

The main building of the mausoleum of Confucius is an architectural and sculptural triumph, representing the faith and creative endeavours of many thousands of followers of the great teacher.
YASUHIRO HAYASHI

A few kilometres outside Luoyang, carved into sandstone cliffs that line the River Yi as it flows towards the Huanghe, are the Longmen Grottoes. Carved into the walls of Dragon's Gate, thousands of Buddhas gaze with calm serenity over the water to the hills on the far side of the river. It is a sculptural wonderland of gods and demons, occupying more than 2000 grottoes and niches carved into the living rock along a kilometre of cliffs. Work began on the grottoes in AD 494 in the reign of Emperor Xiao Wen of the Northern Wei. It continued for more than five centuries under Sui, Tang, the Five Dynasties and Song rule. Generation after generation of artists spent their lives sculpting the endless visage of Buddda out of the solid rock. Over the 1000 years since then, waves of destruction have swept over the land. Barbarians and vandals alike have hacked at the precious relics seeking to destroy the message of the past. There has been fearful damage, but what remains

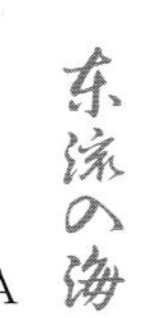

SEIGO OTSUKA

*B*ehind this arched doorway in the Shaolin Temple, sacred to followers of the martial Buddhist arts, is the Dharma cave, inner sanctum for many of the monks whose teaching gave rise to many aspects of Zen Buddhism.

at Dragon's Gate, surmounted by the 17-metre statue of the Vairocana Buddha, is still a stunning treasure.

The people of Shandong are different from their cousins upriver. Their long coastline has given them a maritime tradition which in turn has caused a fire for exploration. When the Qing dynasty in its dying days opened the vast wealth of Manchuria to non-Manchus, it was the men and women of Shandong who swarmed into the provinces that now make up the industrially mighty northeast. It was Shandong men who steered early junks for the Song dynasty (AD 960–1279), and when the British needed sturdy men to fill the ranks of their police force in Hongkong, they turned to their naval base at Weihaiwei for Shandong recruits. Having long contacts with the outside world (the great port of Qingdao was founded by Germans in 1898 and was for years a German colony) has made people of the province more open to new ideas. This was not obvious, however, when at the end of the nineteenth century oppression combined with poverty and a lack-lustre and corrupt government proved too much for even the ancient, patient Chinese peasant to countenance any further, and the men of Shandong arose in what has gone down in history as the Boxer Rebellion. That spark set all North China aflame. Shandong men have long had reputations for fiery tempers.

While Mao Zedong and his army of ragtag veterans of the Long March were still in faraway Yanan, little more than a romantic whisper in the marketplace in most Chinese towns, Shandong sheltered scattered communist guerilla bands. They fought first warlords then Guomindang troops then Japanese invaders then the Nationalists again in the last furious days of the civil war. When Marshal Chen Yi led the Eighth Route Army victoriously down from the Manchuria campaign to liberate Jinan, much of the province was already under local Red control. In the provincial capital, the first thing the communists did was to tear down the old Ming dynasty walls. Local historians lament this enthusiastic celebration of victory; the walls were an important local landmark – and today the moat that surrounded the old walled city has been converted into a round-the-town park, a long green 'lung' of willows and shrubs and flowers which encircles the centre of Jinan like a snake.

They may have torn down city walls but a few kilometres away the soldiers of the People's Liberation Army paused in their pursuit of the Guomindang to help peasants repair the broken and crumbling dykes that lined the Huanghe. Dyke building has been a preoccupation of the peasantry of North China for as long as recorded history. Digs of ancient sites reveal that even before the first attempts in the time of Yu the Great to fence in the river itself, moats and dykes surrounded the villages. Today, across the entire stretch of the North China Plain, the enormous twin dykes run either side of the river.

HIROYUKI USAMI

Gazing with eternal benevolence from a niche in Thousand Buddha Hill outside Jinan, one of a colony of Buddhas watches over the capital of Shandong. The hillside is studded with niches and grottoes, home to hundreds of statues. Many were carved in the Northern Wei and Sui dynasties 1500 years ago. They sit today, serene and judicial, watching over the panorama of the Huanghe plain.

Left

Sculptures from the Longmen Grottoes gaze serenely over the Yi River as they have for centuries. The rock carvings and cave temples here are among China's finest religious artworks.

Upstream from Shandong, in Henan, the dykes are even more impressive. Here, in the very bosom of the good earth of Mother China, is where a group of tribes put down roots and Chinese civilisation first grew. It was at least 25 000 years ago. By 10 000 BC, there was settled farming. By 3000 BC, man could write rough ideographs, and towns grew. But in museums of Henan, including the fascinating permanent exhibition hall of the Yellow River Commission in Zhengzhou, there are illustrated impressions of how the forebears of modern *Homo sapiens* may have looked when they roamed these plains of northern China 850 000 years ago.

Henan refutes all claims by pretenders along the river. It was in this fulcrum province covering 167 000 vital square kilometres where the Yellow River meets the North China Plain that the Chinese people developed into a nation. Xi'an upriver in Shaanxi is regarded as something of a comparative upstart, despite its flaunting of the tomb of Qinshihuang and his terracotta soldiers. Why, in Henan, local officials say with a smile, archaeologists have excavated cities built in the misty Shang dynasty, up to ten centuries before the clay warriors of Xi'an were fired. And under the ruins of towns of the Shang era, there is evidence of even earlier civilised human occupation.

It seems almost impossible to turn the earth in the 200 kilometres of valley between Luoyang and Kaifeng without discovering a relic of one of China's pasts. But because of flood and wind, which have laid down deep carpets of silt and loess, the treasures are often buried deeply. Archaeologists digging for relics around Kaifeng commonly judge that the Ming era, roughly 500 years ago, is to be found under 3 metres of soil, the Song of the eleventh century about 6 metres down. These well-educated guesses would seem to be correct; municipal workers digging a trench for watermains in the centre of Kaifeng in 1986 came across a completely preserved bridge of the Song dynasty. It had been covered by silt in a major flood, archaeologists guessed, as they scraped away the sediment at the bottom of a trench 8 metres deep. When it was carefully exposed, students of art found themselves looking at the famed Bridge of Zhou, centrepiece of one of China's most noted works of art.

Left

Framed by hardy plants that send roots into newly laid silt deposits, the sun sets upriver in the Gulf of Bohai.

Overleaf

Fishermen on the River (early fifteenth century) reveals Chinese artists' abiding interest in the harmony and innate beauty of daily life, where even the most humble and mundane of occupations was accorded respect.

FREER GALLERY/AMERICAN HERITAGE

SEIGO OTSUKA

A detail from a pillar in the Gongxian rock caves

SEIGO OTSUKA

A novice monk lights devotional candles made of butter to bring a warm glow of faith to a hall of the Taer Temple.

ACKNOWLEDGMENTS

In the many months I was actively researching background material for *The Yellow River* I was fortunate indeed to receive advice and assistance from a large number of people. It is impossible for me to thank them all.

To some friends, I am particularly indebted. These include Li Chuwen, Huang Zheng Ming and Ni Xue Lin of the Xinhua office in Hong Kong who were generous in their advice and helpful in completing arrangements for me to meet appropriate officials on my research trips along the banks of the Huanghe. In the Xinhua office in the national capital, He Hualin, a most impressive and capable young man, was an invaluable companion and of great assistance as we tramped about the frozen river in Henan province. The leading cadres of the Henan Provincial Foreign Affairs office, Gui Quanshou, Shen Xishun and Cheng Peng were not only immensely helpful but greatly hospitable. In Shandong, Ms Duan Yijun walked with me across the enormous Yellow River Bridge and engineer Li Zuomo of the Shandong Huanghe River Bureau told me of the centuries of work that went into taming the flood. Upriver in Zhengzhou at the headquarters of the Huanghe River Conservancy Commission, engineers Mou Jinze and Gong Shiyang continued the story of the endless struggle to contain the waters. I owe special thanks to my old friend, the legendary Dr Ma Haide, for sharing with me his recollections of the river and its tributaries in the days when he lived in the cave dwellings of Yanan with the survivors of the Long March.

Back home in Hong Kong, I received much help in my research from the vice-chancellor of the University of Hongkong, Dr Wang Gungwu, and the university's librarian, Ms Mimi Yeung. The chief librarian of the Hongkong Polytechnic, Barry Burton, aided me enormously in collecting little-known documents of Yellow River lore. The assistance of my editorial coordinator, Iris Wong, helped me collate this tremendous selection of background material and my wife, Kit, spent endless hours with me sorting and selecting ancient texts and pictures of the civilisations that have flowered and fallen in the nine provinces along the great river.

In Tokyo, Shigeki Ohyama and I spent exhausting days and nights trying to identify hundreds of photographs; he was magnificent in his patience and enterprise. From Tokyo, too, I would like to thank Kenjiro Kumagai and Nobutaka Nagaoka from JBP, who provided easy access to photographs and photographers, and Tetsuo Kinoshita, who translated Japanese television scripts into English.

The publisher's work was eased by the willing assistance of a group of people: Julie Cooke in Hong Kong, Jane Fraser, Jennie Phillips, Penny Pilmer and Kate Rogers in Sydney, all of whom provided cheerful administrative help. Mick Bagnato gave valuable production advice.

Above all I must record my thanks to the millions of Chinese peasants whose lives are shaped by the rise and fall of the muddy waters of the Huanghe. They were splendid hosts, cheerful companions, good friends.

Overleaf

A Tibetan girl, dressed in her festive finery, in her homeland near the upper reaches of the Yellow River.
YASUHIRO HAYASHI

INDEX

YASUHIRO HAYASHI

*B*edecked with prayer flags and brightly coloured bolts of cloth, a hilltop *obo* near Lake Ngoring bears silent testimony to the faith of the mountain peoples.